COUNTRY CLOCKS

and their London Origins

Yorkshire Clockmakers
The White Dial Clock
Westmorland Clocks and Clockmakers
Lancashire Clocks and Clockmakers

COUNTRY CLOCKS
and their London Origins

Brian Loomes

DAVID & CHARLES
NEWTON ABBOT   LONDON
NORTH POMFRET (VT)   VANCOUVER

ISBN 0 7153 7079 0

Library of Congress Catalog Card Number 75–26361

Set in 11 on 13 Bembo
Photoset and printed
in Great Britain by
REDWOOD BURN LIMITED
Trowbridge & Esher
for David & Charles (Publishers) Limited
Brunel House   Newton Abbot   Devon

Published in the United States of America
by David & Charles Inc
North Pomfret Vermont 05053 USA

Published in Canada

CONTENTS

PREFACE

This book deals essentially with clocks made in the British provinces, but includes the early beginnings of the trade in London, which form an inescapable background. My experience as a dealer in country clocks brought home to me long ago that most existing reference books do not give adequate coverage to clocks of this sort, though they are by far the most numerous type of clock to be met with today. I have read scathing remarks about the 30-hour longcase clock alongside glowing descriptions of 30-hour lantern clocks and an apparent failure to recognise that one was to a large extent merely a regional variation of the other; a misunderstanding of the 'factory' origin of white dial clocks; derogatory remarks about 'Yorkshire' clocks; a failure to appreciate the commonness of repeating work in longcase clocks; all manner of aspects which I meet with every day in handling these clocks, yet which most books either misinterpret or, more agonisingly, fail to mention at all. Carved clock cases were long ago 'written off' without being given any examination.

There is a tremendously wide interest in country clocks; many thousands of people own one, though they may be in no sense 'collectors'. Time and time again such owners ask me the very same questions, often *after* having read a book which failed to answer them. Talk to provincial clock restorers and the answers are the same—standard books have failed to deal adequately with the items with which the restorers most frequently deal.

One is led to believe that this provincial neglect arises from too heavy a concentration on London clocks—an understandable failing. My own genealogical interest in my family led me to look into the life of Thomas

7

Loomes, the London clockmaker, and his relationship with the Froman-teels. Here again was a case where utter confusion existed as to how many Fromanteel clockmakers existed, when they worked, and even what their Christian names were—and this of the most important clockmaking family ever to work in Britain!

The point I am leading up to is that almost all the facts and dates in this book arise from my own original researches, since, only by going to the source records, could I feel reasonably certain that they were correct. If they differ from those in other books, as I know many of my dates do (especially with regard to the Fromanteels and some of their London contemporaries), then this is intentional, and I can only say that I have confidence in my dates.

A number of horological experts have been kind enough to help by pass-ing on to me facts and items from their own researches, and these are ac-knowledged elsewhere. My main intention all along has been to draw on my own research findings and experience, and not to help perpetuate the misconceptions of the past. This will explain why my views may at times be unconventional.

I have tried to keep away from explanations of the mechanics of clock movements; there are already plenty of books that do this excellently and most readers are more concerned with the number of spandrels on a clock dial, than the number of teeth on its wheels. I have also omitted historical details of the time-recorders of the ancient Egyptians, waterclocks, sidereal time laws, and early European monastery clocks, with which many works begin, since, interesting as they may be, they are not only outside the ex-perience of the general reader, but quite irrelevant to the development of British clocks in the Provinces.

I hope this book will help the owner of a provincial clock to understand more fully both the clock and the methods of its maker, and to derive more pleasure from that ownership. If it succeeds in that, it will have fulfilled its main purpose.

In the struggle to cram the essential facts and figures into a book, there is always a danger that the most important aspect of all may be squeezed out—that is the love of clocks for their own sake. To the enthusiast there is a beauty and fascination in all old clocks regardless of type, period or qual-ity—something about them which makes one smile inwardly. There is a compelling fascination, even romance, in the very names of the makers, but with familiarity these become more than mere names. I spend a large proportion of my time studying the records of early clockmakers, living in the past if you like. So much so that sometimes I feel I know some of these men as people. If occasionally I include information, which may seem to be not strictly relevant, it is because I feel that to know something about the daily lives of these men is to help make them more alive to us.

The reader whose appetite for clocks and their history has been whetted might find scope for extending that interest by joining the Antiquarian Horological Society (New House, High Street, Ticehurst, Wadhurst, Sussex), whose quarterly journal contains articles of the highest calibre on a wide range of horological topics from unique museum pieces to the simplest country clocks.

CHAPTER 1
EARLY DAYS

The first makers of 'British' clocks were foreigners. In terms of domestic clocks it is unlikely that many were made in Britain before the late sixteenth century, and those that were were mostly the products of foreign craftsmen from Germany, France and the Low Countries.

Before this time those few who could afford them bought their clocks either directly from Europe or from Europeans who brought their wares here to sell. Even when clockmaking did become established in Britain, it was still in Europe that the highest skills lay. For example as late as 1609 James I purchased from Hans Niloe, a Dutchman, a clock 'with music and motions' at a price of £300. This was an incredible sum in those days, when a shepherd's wages were £2 a year plus board. No doubt it was an exceptional clock.

Prices and wages are very difficult items for us to interpret into our present-day values, but it is important that we try to get some idea from the very outset of what such figures mean, in order that we may have some conception of the market in clocks. If we bear in mind income figures from Gregory King's tables of 1688 it may help. The sum of £300 was far more than a year's income to *all* except the nobility, whilst a clergyman, a shopkeeper and an army officer earned roughly the same at about £50 a year. One person in five was in occasional receipt of parish relief! In those terms we might equate £50 then to perhaps £2,000 today, which means that Niloe's clock cost the equivalent of £12,000 or six years' wages to a shopkeeper. Such clocks could only be for kings!

In the late sixteenth century then, we are concerned with a very small number of clockmakers (less than twenty perhaps) working for a very small market, very few of whose clocks survive. We are unlikely ever to come across clocks by these men except in museums, and, even if we did, they are likely to be just as far out of our financial reach today as they would have been if we had been alive at the time of their construction. For the ordinary person clocks were quite out of the question.

It follows that, at the time we are concerned with here, domestic clockmaking in this country means clockmaking in London. Provincial clocks would be extremely rare, if not totally unknown. Church clocks are, of course, quite different and we are not concerned with those in this book.

Henry VIII and Queen Elizabeth both possessed numerous clocks, probably all of European make. Henry's clockmaker was Nicholas Kratzer, supposedly a Bavarian who was working in England by 1516. Nicholas Urseau, presumed to be a Frenchman, is said to have been at work as early as 1531, and was clockmaker to Elizabeth until he died, probably as a very old man, in 1590. Urseau lived at Charing Cross in 1565, when he brought an action to recover a clock which had been stolen from him. The thief had taken it to a widow who had pawned it for 13s 4d, and Urseau claimed that the pawnbroker knew that it was a stolen clock. Just what sort of clock this was we don't know, nor whether Urseau got it back again, but the pawnbroker must surely have had his suspicions if he offered such a small sum for a clock made by the Royal Clockmaker.

In 1572, perhaps in anticipation of Urseau's retirement or death, a successor had already been chosen (though not yet appointed as is sometimes stated) in Bartholomew Newsam, who is believed to have been the first native British clockmaker. He was officially appointed to succeed Urseau in 1590, but that appointment seems to have been very short-lived. By 1591 another person was appointed, and in any case Newsam died in 1593, so held office for no more than four years at the very most. Two clocks of his survive, one of which is in the British Museum (illustrated in *Clocks in the British Museum* by Hugh Tait), and is said to have been made about 1580–90.

Surprisingly, little accurate information has been published about these early makers. Even their nationalities are for the most part uncertain, as with the next man on our list, Randolph Bull. Whilst his name may sound English enough, this goldsmith and watchmaker is thought to have been

French. The misleading date of 1617 is sometimes given for his royal appointment, but in fact Bull was made clockmaker to the Queen on 27 November 1591 at a salary of 12d a day and £3 6s 8d livery—we should remember this rate of pay for later comparison. Was Newsam old or sick or just out of favour? Whatever the reason, Bull was now Royal Clockmaker. No clock of his seems to have survived, though some of his watches still exist.

It seems to have been every bit as important to have had friends in the right places as to have been skilled at one's craft, in fact at times much more important. Bull survived for ten years after the accession of James I when, in 1613, he was ousted by a court favourite from Scotland. In 1617 Bull was relegated to the position of keeper of the clock at Westminster Palace (not promoted to it, as is sometimes suggested). Bull was saved further embarrassment by dying soon after. Recently I came across his will, made in April 1617 and proved in October. Its contents are unenlightening, except that they tell us that he owned property in Fulham and left a widow and four daughters as well as his son, Emanuel, also a watchmaker. One overseer of the will was Anthony Risby, a watchmaker, who five years later was one of the original petitioners for the Clockmakers' Company.

Among the clockmakers of this period were John Vallin, and his son Nicholas. John, who came from Ryssell (Lille) in Flanders, died in London in 1603. Nicholas died the same year. Several clocks and watches survive by Nicholas, but none, so far as I know, by John. The British Museum has a musical clock by Nicholas dated 1598, the earliest musical clock ever made in this country (illustrated in Hugh Tait's *Clocks in the British Museum*). Contrary to a recently published statement Nicholas Vallin (or Valline) was never Royal Clockmaker.

The Vallins were Huguenot immigrants. Their name derives from Wallon (Walloon) and forms such as Wallin, and Walewyn occur as well as Valline, Vallijn, etc. They were members of the Austin Friars Dutch Church and, like many Huguenot clockmakers, they retained their own language, though no doubt spoke English too.

Perhaps the best-known name of these early clockmakers is that of David Ramsay, and it was he whose appointment as Clockmaker to James I in 1613 was responsible for Bull's downgrading. Ramsay's son, William, later wrote how, on his accession, James sent for his father, then in France. Ramsay was made Groom of the Bedchamber at just over £26 per year and in 1613 Clockmaker at £50 a year, with a pension of £200 a year. In 1616 he was paid £234 10s for purchase and repair of clocks and watches for the King. In 1618 his title was Chief Clockmaker to the King, presumably in view of Bull's death.

The tremendous sums of money lavished on Ramsay contrast sadly with Randolph Bull's shilling a day. The reason was almost certainly because of his social background. He was 'related to the Earls of Holderness' being the brother of Sir James Ramsay, and of George Ramsay, who later became Earl of Dalhousie. This relationship is stated in a document of 1624 which concerns George's alleged breach of promise to marry a girl. He excuses himself on the grounds that the girl, being but 'the daughter of a poor pie-woman', has an unsuitable background.

Some very strange perks were granted to Ramsay as supplementary sources of income. One of them, made in 1625, was a grant in shares of treasure trove in the county of Lincoln. Another, in 1630, was a grant of two parts of 'all pirate goods happening in Ireland for 21 years' to which there was much opposition, 'the like never having been granted to anyone but the Lord Admiral'. In 1626 he was paid £150 for coins to be given to the King on Coronation Day; in 1627 he was paid £441 for clock maintenance; in 1628 £415 for clocks, and so on.

Ramsay was a strange character, obviously keenly interested in all kinds of metallurgy, particularly in precious metals and in mining processes. One of his more unusual exploits was his attempt in 1634 to discover hidden treasure in Westminster Abbey by the use of divining rods. It seems very incongruous today that the age which began the scientific study of time-keeping and was shortly to produce the pendulum regulator, was also one in which a royal officeholder hunted for treasure with divining rods.

Ramsay held the royal appointment for almost half a century, and he probably did it more by virtue of his social connections than his abilities, he seems to me to have been far more of a mechanically minded courtier than a courtly minded craftsman. How many courtiers and brothers of earls attended the bedchamber with engravers' callouses on their hands? Ramsay was probably a workmaster and was far more likely to have supervised the making of clocks by his mostly unknown journeymen (we do know one name—William Pettit), than to have made them himself.

These background considerations are very important in illustrating the nature of clockmaking in these early days. Now a little space must be devoted to the clocks. As we have seen, these clockmakers worked exclusively for royalty and nobility. The prime function of a clock, that of telling the time, was almost subordinated as each craftsman tried to outdo the other in a display of opulent and extravagant ornamentation. The clocks though remained essentially European. If they had no name on them they might well be taken for European examples.

It is suggested even that some of the cases were made in France or Holland, because the engraving work is too good to be English. The Dutch were perhaps the most famous of all engravers at this time. British map- and print-makers of the late sixteenth and early seventeenth centuries almost always employed Dutch engravers on their better works. Quite possibly the same applied to engraving on clock cases, it being done by foreigners resident in London.

Most of these clocks, though not all, are spring-driven table clocks, sometimes called 'drum' clocks. They are of a more delicate and intricate nature than the weight-driven clock, which we shall consider later. Making the springs was also a serious problem in England at this time. Table clocks are of two types: one lies horizontally with its dial facing upwards; the other stands vertically and has its dial in the now more normally accepted position, facing forward. We might liken the position of the dials to those on a present-day watch and clock respectively.

Table clocks were portable, being capable of functioning on surfaces that were not absolutely level. A nobleman might take his timekeeper with him from one room to the next, or when journeying away from home even. The table clock was essentially a richly ornamented and decorative item for a small clientele. It could never thrive in Britain, nor did it, save in very exclusive circles and then for a short period only. Late examples of this type of clock are known, by Edward East and Henry Jones for example, but these are very exceptional.

It was the non-portable weight-driven clock that achieved widespread popularity in England. Clocks that were cheap enough to sell in adequate numbers were essential if clockmakers were to be assured of a living. Clocks had to be substantial enough to stand up to life in a farm-house, not just in a palace. The delicacy, intricacy, opulence, and price of spring-driven table clocks were all direct obstacles to their future. They might be fine for the occasional wealthy customer, or as a showpiece example of what a clock-maker could achieve, but they were unrealistic and never relevant in terms of clocks for the general public. This is not a criticism, as of course they were never *intended* for the public. And whilst the early table clocks were made more as bejewelled trinkets for wealthy patrons or as entertaining automata rather than as mundane timekeepers, they are relevant to our study of clocks because they illustrate the nature of the beginnings of the craft in England and because they set a standard.

The clock of the people began about the beginning of the seventeenth century. It was the weight-driven hanging wall clock, known today as the lantern clock, but at the time called simply a 'brass clock'. Whether its origins can be traced back to Europe or not, it became in a very short time the typically English clock, the kind of clock which everyone, who could afford a clock at all, could buy. A simple lantern clock could be bought in 1656 for as little as £2 10s (two and a half weeks' wages to our shopkeeper), which, if we continue to use our formula of multiplying by forty to reach an approximation in today's values, would make the cost of the clock £100.

The lantern clock was the clock for the wider public. At this time, how-ever, that wider public was very much smaller in proportion to the total population than it was, say, in the nineteenth century, by which time per-haps eight or nine out of every ten homes had a clock. In the early seven-teenth century clocks were new-fangled and costly devices, without which people had always managed and on which only a small proportion of that potentially wide public would be willing to spend money. For those who did want a clock the lantern clock was the only type available to them.

The origin of the name 'lantern' (applied to a clock) is unknown, but is almost certainly much newer than the clock to which it refers. No one seems able to turn up a contemporary reference to them by this name, and any records I have personally seen call them simply 'clocks' or 'brass clocks'; there was no identification problem since these were the only type of clock available. Other names sometimes applied to these clocks include 'bedpost', 'sheepshead', 'Cromwellian', and 'birdcage', but since some of these names are used more frequently to refer to other types of clock, I shall, for purposes of clarity, keep to the term 'lantern'. The term 'bedpost' clock obviously arose from the posted construction principle in a vague way resembling the posts of a four-poster bed. 'Birdcage' similarly stems from the idea of the upright bars round a cage being similar in principle to the posts of a lantern clock. The idea, which I have sometimes seen seriously put forward, that a lantern clock hung on a bedpost, is too ludicrous to discuss. The origin of the term 'lantern clock' from 'latten clock' (ie a clock made of the metal latten) has no foundation in fact. Latten was a different metal from brass and not simply an alternative name for brass.

Lantern clocks one meets with today may have any one of three types of regulating mechanism—balance-wheel, short pendulum or long pendulum. We exclude modern reproduction ones, which are spring driven. An old lantern clock is sometimes found today with a spring-driven movement, but these are ones which have been converted by having their original movements replaced by bracket clock movements—in other words, they have been spoiled. Old lantern clocks were *always* weight driven.

At the time of their introduction, however, they were regulated by one method only, known as the balance wheel (see below). Some European

Balance-wheel, used as a means of regulating lantern clocks. The wheel is made to rotate alternately clockwise and anti-clockwise by impulses to the projecting pallets on its arbor

clocks had a weighted arm, called a foliot, in place of the wheel, but the foliot was not used in Britain. With the weight in position the balance-wheel is pushed first to the left till a lip on its axle (in clock language, a pallet on its arbor) strikes against an approaching tooth of the escape-wheel. Its direction of swing is thereby caused to reverse till the other pallet contacts a tooth on the opposite side of the escape-wheel, and so on, each swing of the wheel causing one beat of the clock, each swing being impulsed by the push of the escape-wheel. It is a primitive and not very efficient system.

The only means of making the clock beat faster or slower was by increasing or decreasing the power force, ie the weight. This was done by adding or removing a little lead shot from the weight canister by trial and error till the correct weight was arrived at. It worked, but was a far from perfect method, and balance-wheel clocks are said to have varied in accuracy by as much as a quarter of an hour a day. This may seem an amusing degree of inaccuracy to us, but to the contemporary owner it did not matter, for this was the most precise time-measurer he had ever known (apart from a sundial). What was rather undesirable was that its inaccuracy could vary from day to day from fast to slow or vice versa with, for instance, such influences as the temperature and weather conditions.

Nevertheless for the early seventeenth-century owner the lantern clock was a wonderful device and was quite sufficient for his needs. He probably was not even aware of its inaccuracy. Moreover, inaccurate though it was, the lantern clock was usually a better time-keeper than the spring-driven table clock, which was inclined to be erratic as the spring unwound, partly due to the quality of the spring, partly to the problem of the tension weakening as it unwound and thereby driving the clock with a force that was not constant. Even later spring-driven clocks with compensating devices could seldom compete with the constancy of the invariable driving-power of weight-driven clocks, the pull of the weight being always the same whether fully wound or almost run-down.

Lantern clocks were made to hang on the wall. Sometimes they were placed on a wooden bracket, though such a bracket made no contribution beyond that of appearance, unless it was that of providing a rigid level platform. The simpler method was to hang it on a large nail knocked into the wall, and some lantern clocks have a steel spike, called a spur, behind each rear 'foot'. These spurs would have dug into the plastered wall and thereby help the clock retain its vertical position.

After developing from the stage where much of the construction was of iron, the lantern clock reached the form, which we would now recognise, by the second quarter of the seventeenth century. There were several different styles of frets around the top of lantern clocks, and these have sometimes been seen as being indicative of period. The present view seems to be generally that one cannot take them as pointers to period. Frets of dolphin pattern, heraldic pattern, and other less recognisable styles appeared, it seems, according to the whim of the maker, or perhaps of the purchaser, rather than at any particular period.

The heraldic type has a shield as a central motif, and this may well have been for the purpose of engraving the coat of arms or perhaps simply the initials of the first owner. Many, however, still have blank shields to this day, as does the one illustrated (see p. 20). Dutch engravers frequently left a blank amongst a group of heraldic shields on, for example, a map of this period, for that very purpose, and it seems to me that a clockmaker who engraved the pattern and hatching on the surface of the whole fret, did not leave the shield unengraved by accident, nor as an aid to the design, but for the purpose of bearing identification marks to be specified by the owner.

I have photographs of five lantern clocks by Thomas Loomes. On two of them he used the heraldic fret (one blank, one with initials I.W. over M.N.—first owner and wife?); on two he used the dolphin fret; on one a leafwork fret. All originally had alarmwork. Four are signed on the dial, one on the fret. Two of the inscriptions read: *Thomas Loomes At The Mermayd In Lothbury* (they differ, however, in the style of engraving), while the others read variously, *Thomas Loomes Londini fecit* (on the fret), *Thomas Loomes at ye Mermayd In Lothbury Londini,* and *Thomas Loomes at ye Maremaid In Lothbury fecit.*

Authorities disagree as to the status of the lantern clock, and some take exception to the statement that it was never an 'aristocratic' clock, yet there is no doubt that its origins and function were humble. It was made as an inexpensive clock, sturdy and reliable enough to enable it to survive the rough usage of everyday life. This very origin made it a clock of the people, not the aristocracy. That it began life in this way, however, did not prevent

Lantern clock by Thomas Loomes, c1655, made 'At The Mermayd In Lothbury'

a certain demand from wealthier patrons for their own grander versions of this humble clock. Hence, examples exist by makers who are better-known for their more spectacular types of clock, men such as Edward East. The customer who could afford it was able to have his lantern clock made more ostentatious by an additional amount of engraving work, by the gilding of the dial, and even by having the chapter ring surfaced with a thin layer of pure silver instead of the normal 'silvered' appearance achieved by the application of silver chloride paste. Therefore, whilst the lantern clock was not aristocratic in type, examples do exist which were aristocratic in finish, appearance and price.

The lantern clock usually had two trains, one for going, one for striking. In the early period these were placed one behind the other, going train in front, and each was driven by its own separate rope-hung weight. Its loud bell made the hour audible throughout the whole house, which was a very important factor in an age when the lantern clock would be the only clock in the house. Early longcase clocks often have loud bells for the same reason. It registered the time by a single hand on the dial, the chapter ring being marked off in half-hour, sometimes quarter-hour, units. Minutes were not marked, since there was no minute hand, and the quarter-hour unit was the smallest fraction that could be registered on such a small dial. Those which show minutes today do so because they have been converted at a later date to carry two hands. The duration of these early clocks would be about twelve hours at one winding, depending on how high the clock was hung on the wall.

The foregoing remarks relate essentially to lantern clocks controlled by the first principle mentioned, the balance-wheel. With the introduction of the pendulum (about 1658, an event which will be dealt with more fully later) one might have expected the balance-wheel principle to have become obsolete overnight, and to a certain extent this did happen. However, some lantern clocks continued to be made with the old balance-wheel even as much as twenty years after 1658, particularly in country areas. The reasons for this are unknown, but it was probably not through ignorance of the new pendulum principle but rather because the balance-wheel lantern was less sensitive to being slightly out of vertical than the pendulum version.

We have already seen how the trade was dominated in London by foreigners—French, German, Dutch, even a Scot. The English clock and watchmakers complained that they could barely survive in the capital of their own land. In 1622 a group of them got together to petition the king, making the following major points: that they found it hard to make a living being undercut in price by foreigners, chiefly Frenchmen, whose workmanship was bad; that the strangers peddled their wares in the houses of the nobility, who were deceived into buying poor quality items, these being only outwardly beautiful; that they even told the customers that they, the foreigners, were the ones who really made the clocks onto which English sellers put their names, and that the customers might have identical goods more cheaply by buying direct from them, the true makers; that the foreigners not only lived in small apartments at cheap rents, but even kept shops and took on apprentices, who were trained into poor craftsmen; that the foreigners far outnumbered the native craftsmen. They asked that the laws in force abroad be applied in England, namely that no foreigners should be allowed to work except under a native master and that no foreign work should be imported.

The petitioners were sixteen in number. Headed by Robert Grinkin they were: Henry Archer, Ferdinando Garret, James Vautrolier, Edmund Bull, George Bull, Francis Forman, Isaac Simes, John Smith, John Wellowe, Anthony Risbie, William Yate, Nicholas Walters, Cornelius Yate, Daniel Saunders, John Harris. The foreigners they complained of numbered forty-six and were listed by name. Top of that list should perhaps have been David Ramsay, but the petitioners had more sense than to point the finger at the king's clockmaker. They did, however, go so far as to list one William Petitt, working 'with Mr Ramsay in Tutle Street, King's clockmaker'. They also listed 'Josias Cuper, Lord Dorset's page', who was a Frenchman.

The fact that almost all the royal clockmakers, including the present one and his workman, had been foreigners, the bulk of them French, was hardly likely to warm the king to this petition, and apparently he ignored it, for nothing happened. What is not generally realised in connection with this protest, is that it was not just the clockmakers who were growing resentful of foreigners. Many other trades were equally incensed. In that same year, in quick succession, came similar protests first from the Goldsmiths' Company concerning no less than 183 alien goldsmiths, from the coopers concerning alien coopers employed by foreign brewers, from the warehouse keepers and from the leatherdressers—all of them were getting worked up about foreigners taking their trade.

The clockmakers must have felt especially resentful of men like Ramsay and Cuper, whose positions seem to have come through social connections rather than through merit. It may not be insignificant that two of the petitioners were named Bull, perhaps related to Randolph, the man who had been deposed in favour of Ramsay. Another was Anthony Risby, known friend of the now deceased Randolph Bull. Ramsay was certainly not a popular figure in those circles. In such a small, close-knit group, friendships and hostilities were especially important.

The petition's claim that the foreigners were falsely representing themselves as the real craftsmen of the trade, reminds us of the essentially European style of much clockwork of this time, and it is by no means impossible that a number of native traders did simply add their names to a foreign product.

Various manoeuvres culminated in a second petition being presented, at the end of 1629, to the new king, by the now larger body of London clockmakers, asking for incorporation as a Company. The Charter of Incorporation was granted on 22 August 1631. An essential factor in the reasons behind the forming of the Company was the objection of the locals to 'alien' workers, but of course it was a matter of opinion as to who *was* an alien, especially amongst the many Flemish-speaking clockmakers. Josias Cuper for example, a French clockmaker and one of the aliens named in the 1622 petition, had become a freeman of the Blacksmiths' Company in 1628 by virtue of which he presumably considered himself now a native clockmaker. Ironically in 1631 he is one of the new subscribers to the charter designed to keep out aliens!

The original subscribers, as these first members were called, were very largely a group of London-domiciled 'aliens' who banded together to keep out new immigrants. The first Master, appointed for life, was not surprisingly David Ramsay, the courtier from Scotland. The number of Anglo-Saxon names among this group is very small indeed. It has been said that with the forming of the Clockmakers' Company both English and alien clockmakers became united. The domination of the Company in its early years by courtiers and anglicised Frenchmen seems to me to be a feature far more likely to lead to dissension than unity, and the most outstanding facet of the early years is the constant bickerings, jealousies, and allegations between the one master, three wardens and ten assistants on the one side and their members on the other.

The regulations were long, complicated and at times hard for the members. They were, however, heavily loaded with exemptions for the office-holders, who for the most part were able to bend the rules when it suited them. No one could practise the trade unless accepted into the Company, when he must agree to its rules restricting the number of apprentices allowed, and then take only those approved by the Company, must pay his subscription, attend meetings, lay his shop and goods open to inspection by Company officers, who would search for inadequate workmanship and confiscate any sub-standard goods. The rules were intended to maintain

23

high standards, and in that aim were both necessary and justified. It was in the application of them that troubles arose and the early days of the Company were often stormy.

At times there was strong resentment of the firm enforcement of the rules, even from men who had supported the forming of the Company, men such as Lewis Cooke. He was working in York as early as 1614, where his work was very highly thought of, and one could hardly expect a Yorkshireman to be anything but outspoken. The trouble was that he had taken on an apprentice (John Da⁻erill) without permission six months earlier (1631). Cooke first refused to attend the court, then, when forced to attend, he refused to pay not only the fine but also told the court he would not now pay the 40s subscription, which he had originally promised towards the cost of the charter. After addressing the court 'in a very abusive and scornfull manner with much ill language' he left. At the same court one Mr Reco was 'forbidden to work any longer in the trade of a clockmaker'. In 1639 John Drake was in trouble for having bound an apprentice through the Blacksmiths' Company (the former practice), when of course he was now supposed to do this through the Company of Clockmakers. These early teething troubles were perhaps to be expected.

Two of the main offenders against the Company were named Fromanteel and Loomes. Let us look briefly at the background of the latter first. The premises known by the sign of the Mermaid in Lothbury were already established as a clockmaking house before the formation of the Clockmakers' Company. William Selwood was master of this business. His prime output seems to have been lantern clocks, of the type already discussed. Selwood became free of the Clockmakers' Company in 1633. He was a bachelor, and lived and worked with his brother, John, who was free in 1640. Three more brothers followed different trades. John Selwood married in 1642 to Dorothy Brookes, who may well have been related to Thomas Loomes, whom John took as apprentice about this time. Loomes himself became a free brother in 1649 and when John Selwood died in 1651, Thomas Loomes was able to step in to fill his place and was eventually allowed by the Company to take over Selwood's young apprentices, still not fully trained.

Two years later William Selwood also died, which left Thomas Loomes in sole charge of the Mermaid. At the early age of about twenty-six he was

24

master of a thriving business, with a multiplicity of apprentices and journeymen taken over from the two Selwood brothers, as well as his own.
Trying to keep track of these apprentices was extremely difficult and
Loomes was in constant trouble with the Clockmakers' Company. The
confusion was made worse by the practice of 'turning over' an apprentice.
A clockmaker who was under quota might take on an apprentice 'for' some
other maker who was over-staffed, and later would 'turn him over' when
that second maker was allowed, or could get away with, the extra apprentice.

For instance, Richard Beck was apprenticed in 1646 to Thomas Alcock
and was later turned over to John Selwood, who died in 1651. On 16
December 1651 the Company ordered that Loomes must not take on Beck
until permission had been sought from the Company. The necessary permission was granted on 5 January following. In 1653 Beck was free of his
apprenticeship, but Loomes had jumped the gun by allowing him to sign his
own clocks before he had been officially recognised as a freeman. Loomes
was fined at the very same court meeting which accepted Beck as a freeman.

All this must have been extremely aggravating to an impatient young
man trying hard to run a business. One can see that the Company was doing
its best to stop the abuse of too many apprentices being shunted around too
few masters, a practice which was probably practised deliberately on occasions to camouflage exactly how many apprentices a particular master
had at any one time. From Loomes's point of view, however, it must have
looked as though the Company was so hampered by its regulations that the
tail was wagging the dog. Tom Loomes and many others felt very strongly;
so did the wardens of the Company. Matters were soon to come to a head.

As with many historical disputes we cannot always be sure today which
party was in the right. In 1656 a considerable body of freemen of the Company drew up a petition to the Lord Mayor, complaining about the way in
which the Company's affairs were conducted by the Court of Assistants,
that is the Master, Wardens and Assistants of the Company, whose decisions
on Company matters were final. Numerous grievances are listed including:
their lack of a hall for holding meetings, which were at that time conducted
in taverns 'and such disorderly places'; that whilst the Company was
formed to keep out foreigners, Frenchmen were 'admitted to rule the Free-

man'. If we consider that the office of Master rotated amongst only five men at this time, we may see further grounds for complaint. The Master was: 1645, Edward East; 1648 and 1649, Robert Grinkin; 1650 and 1651, Simon Bartram; 1652, Edward East again; 1653, John Nicasius; 1654, Grinkin again; 1655, Nicasius again . . . after which the surnames appear more obviously English. These men seem to have been part of a clan, for as we shall see later Grinkin and Nicasius were good friends. They further complained that too many apprentices were permitted with the result that they 'fear the end of their service would be the beginning of beggary'; and that attempts to discuss this with the assistants met with no response. All told, the complainants now found themselves 'in a worse condicion than ever we were before the Charter was granted'. There were thirty-three signatories (plus another three in the margin). They were:

Simon Dudson	Thomas Hollis	Thomas Loomes
Humfrey Pierce	Thomas Claxton	Richard Taylor
Francis Bowen	Thomas Weeks	Richard Ricord
William Godbud	Jon (———)	John Drake
Job Betts	Robert Lochard	Nicholas Higginson
Wm Almond	Samuel Vernon	John Matchett
Ralphe Ashe	John Thorne	William Comfort
Henry Erbery	Ahasuerus Fromanteel	Thomas Daniel
Henry Kent	Richard Beck	Joseph Munday
Lancelot Meredith	Andrew Prime	John Waffield
Samuel Horne	Thomas Moth	Thomas (Pate?)

We will look more closely at this group in a moment.

It looks as if the Lord Mayor wished to avoid involvement and they seem to have been sent away to try to sort it out among themselves, for a meeting was held on 8 September 1656. This failed to resolve anything and next a counter-petition was presented to the Lord Mayor by other freemen, who were evidently put up to it by the Assistants. The Assistants themselves also gave their reply to the Lord Mayor. These replies are too lengthy to go into in detail, but it is evident from reading them that the Assistants were far from innocent of all the charges. It is interesting to examine the counter-petition, which exists in two versions, a rough copy and a neat one. Those who signed the neat copy were fourteen in number:

Thomas Taylor	Jerimie Gregory
Edmund Grinkin	Edward Hollidaie
Jeremie East	Francis Mathew
Evan Jones	William Clay
David Moodie	Robert Robinson
Henry Erbery	John Cooke
Ambrose Blisse	Isaack Daniell

However, on the rough copy there were a further five signatures of men of much more importance, who seem to have changed their minds and withdrawn their support before the document was submitted. These five were: Robert Grinkin, Edward East, Onisephorus Helden, John Bayes and John Harris. These men, comprising as they did a part of the administration of the Company and therefore being amongst those chiefly complained against, could hardly sign a counter-petition that was meant to appear to come from independent rank and file members. However, the presence of their names on the rough copy indicates that they played no small part in drumming up this 'unprompted' support.

Let us consider briefly who some of these petitioners were, for it may help to clarify the whole business. The rebels who complained included no less than three who were subsequently to become Masters, and several with seniority of membership superior to any of the 'administration'. Apart from Fromanteel there was his son-in-law, Thomas Loomes, and his brother-in-law, Andrew Prime. Richard Beck and Simon Dudson were former Loomes apprentices. Richard Ricord was probably the Mr Reco expelled in 1632 (but re-admitted in 1649). John Drake we have noticed was in trouble with the court earlier, although as a warden of the Blacksmiths' Company he was a man of some standing. Henry Erbery we can discount, as he signed for *both* sides. John Matchett was later suspended for being a Catholic. In short they might seem to have been a group of malcontents stirred up by Fromanteel and his family, a group of relatives, friends, and fellow-sufferers in adversity. Yet it would be quite wrong to dismiss them, as the Wardens tried to do, as a group of mere troublemakers, for they included men of considerable merit, skill and experience.

As to the administration and their supporters, firstly they were almost all of them makers of watches rather than clocks, fine watches, superb watches, but because of their association in this wealthier luxury market they were perhaps inclined to clan together. Of the twelve signatories the top five, who were the administration proper, felt they must withdraw to give a semblance of spontaneity to the document. This left only seven names, against the thirty-six rebel signatories, and two of that seven were not even members of the Company at all (Edmund Grinkin and William Clay)—a fault of which the administration had accused the rebels! A little scratching around raised a further seven, making fourteen in all, if we count Henry Erbery, who wanted to please both sides at once. Even then they were scraping the barrel.

What do we know of the administration? First, there was Robert Grinkin, an excellent watchmaker. It is not normally appreciated that there were two men of this name. The first was Master of the Blacksmiths' Company in 1609 (although of course a watchmaker, not a blacksmith) and an original 1622 petitioner, but he had died in 1626. In his will he left his mathematical books and his working instruments to his son, Robert, and it is this Robert who was Master of the Company no less than three times in eight years between 1648 and 1655. It is hardly surprising that Edmund Grinkin was a counter-petitioner, being the brother of Robert Grinkin the younger, though Edmund was *not* a freeman of the Company and had no right to sign at all (he was free of the Blacksmiths' Company in 1637). Of Edward East I shall write later, but it was hardly pure chance that Jeremy East was a signatory as he must surely have been a relative of Edward. Indeed in 1662 Edward and Jeremy worked side by side in Fleet Street, alongside John Nicasius and David Moodie. William Clay was not a member of the Company and had no right to sign. John Cooke had formerly been apprenticed to Cornelius Mellin, one of the very aliens against whom the Company had been formed. Francis Mathew had only just that very year been made a freeman, and was obviously simply doing as he was told. Of the rest, John Bayes and Jeremy Gregory were good friends of Grinkin, each had been left a gold ring in his will in 1660, and he called them his 'very loving friends'.

John Nicasius was also named amongst Grinkin's friends in his will, and it is perhaps to his credit that he did not sign even the rough draft.

Therefore, whilst we can recognise certain family connections on the part of the rebels, we can see that the counter-petitioners were much more deeply involved in advantageous friendships and relationships, and that far from representing the rank and file, the counter-petition was a very prejudiced and discreditable document.

The administration had tried to discredit the rebels by saying that the latter could not be worse off now than before the charter, since none of them was working in the trade at that time. This is, of course, totally irrelevant, apart from being untrue, and further invalidates the administration reply. In fact several of the rebels had seniority in the trade as freemen dating from the 1630s, whilst not one of the fourteen counter-petitioners was free before 1640.

The petitioners were not satisfied and wrote to the Lord Mayor to say so, asking for a fair deal for the 'greate number of Artists made poor by these grievances'. We can only assume that the Lord Mayor gave all parties a good talking-to, and it seems they all gave assurances to try to redeem the situation.

The Company ultimately decided to make an example of Tom Loomes, whom they reported to the Lord Mayor for having *five* apprentices instead of the permitted two, and on 25 February 1656/7 the Mayor ordered him to comply. Fromanteel, never one to bear injustice uncomplainingly, also attended the meeting and seems to have rather lost his composure there, so much so that he felt obliged to write and apologise later and his letter, dated 3 March 1656/7, is preserved amongst the Clockmakers' Company archives. The letter is a model on how to insult one's enemy whilst apologising to him.

Things had been said on both sides, he wrote, that 'did not become Christians nor Civil men', and he rebuked himself for having told the Assistants that his journeyman could do more than any five of them together. He confessed that he ought not to have said that—although it was true! He was falsely accused of having taught the trade to Henry Creek (not apprenticed through the Company); of having 'taken a mere smith that was never trained up in clockwork and (having) taught him the trade'; that his son

(-in-law), Loomes (sometimes misread as Louis, this giving rise to the appearance of a wholly fictitious Louis Fromanteel in some authors' lists), had three apprentices more than he ought—and yet his son had no apprentice other than those that had been approved by the Company (except, he admitted, some belonging to other masters). He ended by noting that some freemen, however, did plainly abuse the rules, Messrs Ireland, Davis and Miller, to mention but a few.

Satisfying as this letter may have been to its writer, the outcome was the same—on 27 April Tom Loomes was fined 40s. It was neither the first, nor the last, time the two were to be in trouble.

It does seem as if the rebels were justified in complaining about some of the abuses, though it may well be true that they were roused not so much because the rules were being broken, but because others got away with it whilst they did not. We must remember that the body of London clock-makers at this time was still small, probably less than 150. By 1662 they numbered 168. They would all be known to each other, many were related, and apart from bonds of relationship other bonds of a political and religious nature were bound to form, as we shall shortly see.

We may sometimes wonder, amid all the intrigue, petitions and court sessions, how they ever found time to actually make clocks or watches, but of course they did, and some became very prosperous. Robert Grinkin, for example, seems to have been the last of the family; he died childless in 1661, requesting that he be buried alongside his brother, Edmund. His tools he passed in his will to his brother (-in-law?), Austin Banks, and these tools were not inconsiderable: 'my great and best deviding plate of brass and my best oylestone . . . my best vices, equalling tongues and plyers and all my vices'. He also had a considerable library of books, including some on mathematics inherited from his father, and he left a selection of a dozen of his best volumes to his brother-in-law, Francis Hanslapp (the Hanslapp family included several clockmakers).

Grinkin's will even gives a rare glimpse of a man's appearance, at least of the clothes he wore. He left to his servant: 'my . . . suite and cloake, blacke silke stockings with garters and shooties [shoe ties = laces?] as also my stuffe suite and coate sett forth with silver and gold fringe and coloured silke stockins, garters, shootyes and gloves, two of my best wearing shirts, fower of my best bands with ruffs . . .' Grinkin must have been quite a dandy in those Puritan days.

After the troubles with Fromanteel and Loomes, the Clockmakers' Company seems to have functioned more smoothly. Naturally the officials still tried to stamp out any infringements of the rules, and John Nicasius, a former Master, was in trouble several times, especially for using strong language to the Master.

Part of the duty of the Company officials was to prevent shoddy work being sold by its members and they were entitled to enter premises and search out such deficient works. In 1652 Samuel Davis had an inadequate clock seized. In 1661 a movement was likewise seized 'which was judged not merchantable ware nor fit to be sold until good and mended'. The Company also controlled certain types of instruments and measures. In 1668 Samuel Morris, who worked 'at the sign of the Dripping Pan near Charing Cross', had some faulty rulers confiscated. Men such as John Sellers, the famous globe and map-maker, also became freemen of the Company if, as in his case, they also made instruments for measuring. It is interesting to note that in 1682 the Company confiscated a number of faked clocks with fictitious names, 'all which names are greatly suspected to be invented or fobbed'. In an effort to tighten up on this sort of faking, an Act was passed in 1698 making it compulsory for the maker to sign his name and place on his clocks. In the north clockmakers took little notice and carried on as they always had done. The history of the Clockmakers' Company is interesting in itself, but its importance in this book is the vital part it played in setting standards and controlling them, and the ultimate influence it had in uniting the members of the trade.

What we can learn from the Company's records of the lives of men like Fromanteel and Grinkin is important in helping us to understand the whole picture. We might otherwise easily imagine these men as watchmaking machines, faceless robots who were skilled with the file. That they had friends, enemies, quarrels, brushes with authority, losses of temper, faulty goods impounded, fancy silk stockings with garters—all these things must surely make them more real to us and help us see their works in the setting in which, and for which, they were made.

CHAPTER 2

THE FROMANTEELS

The Fromanteel family headed by Ahasuerus, the founder of the clockmaking line, made what was probably the greatest single contribution to British
horology. They totally changed the nature of the household clock in
Britain, reshaping it into a form which was to remain essentially unchanged
for 200 years. In other words, every antique household clock we are likely
to meet with is a direct descendant of the Fromanteel prototypes; that is
how important they were.

The published information on this, the most important British clockmaking family of all time, is scanty and for the most part inaccurate. No serious
research seems to have been attempted on them until Dr R. Plomp published a paper in *Antiquarian Horology* in September of 1971. It was this excellent start which prompted me to look further into the problem. The
information in this chapter comes mostly from my own researches. There
was so much to be discovered about them, that it is difficult to know what
to leave out.

It has been said that Ahasuerus Fromanteel came to England from Holland. In fact quite the reverse is true, in that he later went to Holland from
England. He was an English-born son of an English-born father of a Fle-
mish-born grandfather, who probably came to England seeking religious
refuge. Ahasuerus was born in Norwich in 1607, the son of Murdoch Fromanteel, a woodturner and chairmaker. The community of Flemish protes-
tant immigrants in East Anglia were known as 'Dutch'. By the 1590s there
were some 5,000 of them in Norwich alone. Integration into the community was slow, and initially they had their own church and language.

Eight-day clock by A. Fromanteel, London, c1680

As well as the 'Dutch' settlement at Norwich there was a similar one at Colchester in Essex and also in London. Most of the 'Dutch' community made their living from the cloth trade with Europe. The importance of this very brief summary of the family's immigrant background will emerge in due course.

Ahasuerus was born on 25 February 1606–7, and was baptised on 8 March in the Dutch Reformed Church at Norwich. He seems to have been the eldest child. His parents, Murdoch and Leah, had five other children, who were: Daniel, born 1610, a tailor in Norwich; Samuel, born 1612, a wood-turner like his father, also in Norwich; John, born 1615, a silk merchant in London; Esther, born 1611, later married John Lakins; Elizabeth, born about 1620, later married to Andrew Prime, a clockmaker in London and Norwich and himself a member of the 'Dutch' community. The nature of

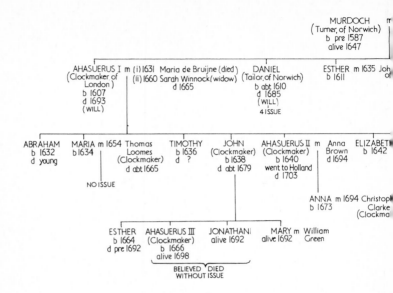

this immigrant community was such that family relationships and friendships were very important, more so than with an ordinary English family. They maintained strong bonds of loyalty, married amongst themselves, and the result was that a tremendously complex pattern of intermarriages and relationships built up over the generations.

Of Ahasuerus's early years we know nothing. He was trained in Norwich, probably as a blacksmith, as it is unlikely that any domestic clockmaker worked there at this time. The spring of 1629 was exceptionally fine and sunny and on Friday, 19 June 1629, Ahasuerus obtained a letter from his minister recommending him to the Dutch Church community in London. That same day one was also issued to Samuel de Gans. The two young bachelors probably travelled together. (Ahasuerus's brother Samuel later married Susanna Gans, who was probably Samuel Gans's sister.) Fromanteel was settled in London in time to experience the city's rejoicings at the birth of the heir to the throne, Charles II born 29 May 1630, an event that was to

34

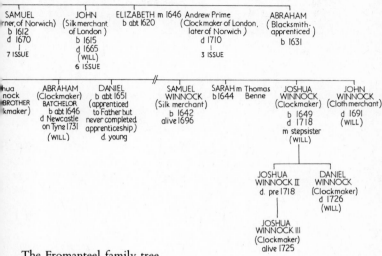

SAMUEL	JOHN	ELIZABETH m 1646	Andrew Prime	ABRAHAM
rner, of Norwich)	(Silk merchant	b abt 1620	(Clockmaker of London,	(Blacksmith-
b 1612	of London)		later of Norwich)	apprenticed)
d 1670	b 1615		d 1710	b 1631
|	d 1665		|	
7 ISSUE	(WILL)		3 ISSUE	
	6 ISSUE			

hua	ABRAHAM	DANIEL		SAMUEL	SARAH m Thomas	JOSHUA	JOHN
nock	(Clockmaker)	b abt 1651		WINNOCK	b 1644 Benne	WINNOCK	WINNOCK
BROTHER	BATCHELOR	(apprenticed		(Silk merchant)		(Clockmaker)	(Cloth merchant)
kmaker)	b abt 1646	to Father but		b 1642		b 1649	d 1691
	d Newcastle	never completed		alive 1696		d 1718	(WILL)
	on Tyne 1731	apprenticeship)				m stepsister	
	(WILL)	d. young				(WILL)	

JOSHUA	DANIEL
WINNOCK II	WINNOCK
d. pre 1718	(Clockmaker)
	d 1726
	(WILL)

JOSHUA
WINNOCK III
(Clockmaker)
alive 1725

The Fromanteel family tree

have no small bearing on his own later life.

By the beginning of the next year, January 1630/1, Ahasuerus was already established as a clockmaker in East Smithfield when he applied to join the Blacksmiths' Company. He was accepted a month later after having produced his apprenticeship certificate to prove that he was fully trained. In August of that year the charter was granted for the formation of the Clockmakers' Company, but Ahasuerus was busy with more important matters in making arrangements for his wedding, which took place on 29 September 1631 at Austin Friars (Dutch) Church in London. The bride was Maria de Bruijne from Colchester, a member of the 'Dutch' community there, where Ahasuerus had relatives and strong connections even before this time. It was not until 29 November 1632, a few weeks after Maria had given birth to their first child, Abraham, who was to die young, that Ahasuerus signed for admittance to the Clockmakers' Company.

By the time their second child, Maria, was baptised (1634), Ahasuerus's mother was in London, for she signed as a witness to the baptism, though her visit may have been only a short one. That same year his sister, Esther, came to London to marry and settle. In 1637 brother Daniel moved to London, in 1639 his father, Murdoch, and younger sister, Elizabeth, also moved to London, and in 1641 brother John married in London. By now all the family had moved there, but brothers Daniel, the tailor, and Samuel, the turner, returned to Norwich to run their own businesses there.

Ahasuerus had been the advance guard of this family migration. The success that he met with must have provided the stimulus which attracted the rest of the family, even his parents, to follow him. By the outbreak of the Civil War Ahasuerus was prospering. However, his is not the romantic story of the penniless boy trudging barefoot to London to seek his fortune. He came from a background of prosperous traders, came with introductions to the right people and fitted in at once among the London 'Dutch' community. But it was not by mere good luck that he prospered—there is no doubt that he also worked hard.

This London community of the Dutch Church—the French, Walloons, Flemings—these were the people amongst whom were found the top clockmakers in the land. Names such as Bull, Urseau, Vallin, Nouwe and Cuper, all appear among Dutch Church families. The Vallins had been members of Austin Friars Dutch Church. These were the surnames also which belonged to the category of 'foreigners', on account of whose domination of the trade had arisen the formation of the Clockmakers' Company.

When the Civil War broke out Ahasuerus was thirty-five. Edward East, a goldsmith/watchmaker' was forty and David Ramsay (who had once been the most powerful clockmaker in the land) had turned fifty and was out of office, with his late master. These three names dominate all others at this time. Some miles away in a Bedfordshire village a three-year-old child played in his father's smithy—his name, Thomas Tompion, was destined to dominate the latter years of the century. Even without the dazzling stars of Ramsay, East and Tompion to block the way, Ahasuerus Fromanteel would never have reached the heights of Royal Clockmaker, for reasons quite other than ability or knowledge.

As the Civil War opened there was only one side to which Ahasuerus might belong, and it was not the side of the King. His origins, religion and upbringing all put him firmly in the Parliamentarian camp, along with most others in East Anglia and London. I do not believe that Fromanteel was especially keen to involve himself in politics. His main concern was with his business and family. However, he was a man of firm individual convictions and on occasions was perhaps too ready to express them in hasty words, which he later regretted. If we are charitable we might see this as making him a more human character, and perhaps more likeable than one whose views swayed more easily with the tide of preferment.

By 1642 Ahasuerus had produced seven children, baptised at Austin Friars Church. They were: Abraham, born 1632, died young(?); Maria, born 1634, later married a clockmaker; Timothy, born 1636, died young(?); John, born 1638, became a clockmaker; Ahasuerus, born 1640, became a clockmaker; Elizabeth, born 1642, married a clockmaker. Three other children were born later: Esther, born 1644, died young; Abraham, born about 1646, became a clockmaker; Daniel, born about 1651, trained as a clockmaker. In fact each one of his surviving sons became a clockmaker, each daughter married one. There must have been one fairly pronounced topic of conversation in that household.

Ahasuerus was soon to sever his allegiance to the church of his youth. Four letters are preserved which he wrote between 1645 and 1646 to the church elders, from which it is apparent that he had been attending meetings of the Anabaptists. Evidently he decided to turn away from his own church, and it is significant that his two youngest children were not baptised there, and indeed probably were not baptised at all. About this time his brother, John, the silk merchant, resident now in Katherine Wheel Alley alongside his married sister, Esther Lakins, also seems to have broken his connection with the church. Their married sister, Elizabeth Prime, and the rest of the family still attended, however, as did their father, Murdoch.

There is great importance in this leaning to the Anabaptist teachings. The minor religious sects such as the Anabaptists sheltered under the wing of the Independents in Parliament, one of whom was named Oliver Cromwell. The New Model Army was formed from the ranks of religious enthusiasts of Independent and Presbyterian leanings. The Parliamentary side were glad enough of the Anabaptist support at this time, but not many years were to pass before their leaders were imprisoned for public speaking and were regarded as almost as serious a threat as the Royalists. Considerable troubles were in store for Anabaptists, as Ahasuerus was soon to find out. There was extensive political intrigue involved among members of the Fromanteel family, not all of it readily understandable to us today.

In January 1649, two weeks before Charles I was executed, Thomas Loomes was admitted a free brother in the Clockmakers' Company. (Two years later John Fromanteel, Ahasuerus's eldest son, was apprenticed to him.) In the Company's ranks, as elsewhere at this time, political differences were fermenting, perhaps between the older freemen with allegiances to the King and the rebels with Parliamentary leanings. We have already seen how Ahasuerus Fromanteel and Thomas Loomes were at the centre of the unrest within the Company.

In 1654 the names of Thomas Loomes and Ahasuerus Fromanteel were to be even more closely connected. Two of a kind politically, united in rebellion against the limitations imposed by the Company, they now became related more closely still when on 18 July Thomas married Ahasuerus's daughter, Mary, at St Saviour's Southwark.

In 1654 Edward East took a young lad as apprentice named Henry Jones. About this time a country blacksmith named Tompion began to serve his apprenticeship. Names such as Tompion and Jones were destined to rise to fame, but now, just as Fromanteel was coming to prominence, they were infants. The highspot of this particular period came for Ahasuerus in 1655 when an unprecedented thing happened: the Court Books of the Clockmakers' Company recorded the following brief entry—'14th January 1655[/6]. Ahasuerus Fromantle was admitted a freeman of the City of London and a free clockmaker'.

In the past this seems to have been skipped over as a freedom entry of a *second* Ahasuerus, but the entry is quite plain. He was made a freeman of the City, not just of the Company—of course he had been a member of the Company for twenty-three years. Checking the records of the Court of Aldermen was found the entry; 1655/6: 'Upon the letter [now apparently lost] of his Highness the Lord Protector in the behalfe of Ahasuerus Fromanteel for the obteyninge of his freedome of the Citie it is ordered by this Courte that the said Fromanteel shall be admitted into the Freedom of this

38

Cittie by redemption in the Companie of Clockmakers payinge to Mr.
Chamblein to the Cittie's use the summe of 46s 8d.'

What this means is that he was allowed to buy his freedom of the city on
payment of 46s 8d, by virtue of being free of the Clockmakers' Company.
City freedom had to come by way of sponsorship by the trading company,
and freedom of that company was a prerequisite to this. In 1632 Fromanteel
had been 'admitted' into the Company, but the term 'freeman' was not
used, as strictly speaking he was a 'free brother', having been transferred
from the Blacksmiths' Company. It looks as if the push from Cromwell personally was the real reason for the City freedom. Indeed his relationship with
the administering officers of the Company were such that he would be the
last person that they would sponsor for such honour. He was made a freeman of the City *despite* the Company rather than by virtue of it—but why?
What had Fromanteel done to merit the personal influence of Cromwell?
Did this preferment come through political motives? It seems possible.

Did it suit Cromwell to be seen to have a protégé under his wing, just as
Charles had had? What other reason could there be? Had Fromanteel produced some great work to prove his excellence to the Protector? If so, then
we know nothing about it today. And yet could it be by pure chance that
Cromwell selected for preferment the very man, who alone out of all his
contemporaries was to revolutionise clockmaking in this country within
two years? There is more than a hint here that Fromanteel may have produced some clock about this time of considerable importance. We cannot
guess what it might have been. However, it seems to me to be by no means
impossible that there might be a connection between this helping hand from
Cromwell in 1655 and the pattern of events which followed in quick succession only two years later.

So far we have concentrated on Fromanteel's life story rather than his
clocks. This is because his life at this time is much more interesting than his
clocks, which can be summed up in a single sentence. So far he had made
ordinary lantern clocks, no better or worse than those made by Thomas
Loomes or any of the 100 other men whose lantern clocks survive from this
period. No clock of his survives, it seems, to compare with the spectacular
products of the Vallins, Newsams or David Ramsay, who was still alive at
this time. Of course he could hardly have had patronage from royalty when

his political views and activities were very anti-Royalist. Without the wealthy patrons to buy them, he could not afford to spend his time on dazzling royal jewellery items. We would expect him to have made very few table clocks, if any.

However, one clock survives which shows that he had the ability if not the patronage. A table clock exists signed *A. Fromanteel fecit* and *E. East*—on the left and right hand sides of the base respectively. It has been suggested that Fromanteel was the engraver and East the maker, but to me it would seem sensible to assume the opposite. We know that East was a goldsmith/engraver; the word *fecit* usually applies to the *maker* who would normally get prior billing to the engraver, as here. Moreover, the left-hand side is traditionally the position for the name of the artist or conceiver of a work of art (such as an engraving) while the right-hand side is traditionally where the engraver gets his credit. I think it is significant that these two men of conflicting political views collaborated and assume that the reason was that East was acceptable in high circles where Fromanteel was not. I cannot picture them collaborating out of friendship. East needed Fromanteel's genius; Fromanteel needed East's acceptability to wealthy patrons. The collaboration clock would seem to date about 1640. I know of no earlier clock by East of this calibre—we must remember he was primarily a watchmaker. The fact that East became Master of the Clockmakers' Company in 1645 must indicate that he was not so politically unacceptable in the Cromwellian camp as the former master ('for life'), Mr Ramsay, who at this time, when Royal Clockmakers were not in great demand, was conspicuous by his absence. Indeed Ramsay seems never to have played much part in the running of the Company.

The collaboration of Fromanteel and East was probably short lived, as are many marriages of convenience. After this initial collaboration I doubt whether either thought he had need of, or time for, the other. By 1656 Fromanteel and East were in quite opposite camps in their attitude to the Clockmakers' Company, and the likelihood is that the gap between them widened with time, not least for political reasons.

On 3 September 1657 John Fromanteel, Ahasuerus's eldest son, entered the service of Salomon Coster in the Hague, where he remained until May 1658. Coster was a clockmaker, who on 16 June 1657 had been granted sole rights for twenty-one years to make and sell clocks in the Netherlands, on the newly devised principle of Christian Huygens of Zulichem. Huygens did not 'invent' the pendulum. What he did was to adapt its use to controlling the timekeeping of a clock. He claimed that his first working model was finished just before Christmas of 1656. Huygens published his findings in September 1658 in a work called *Horologium*, in order to establish that he was the inventor—and he pointed out that already others were making modified versions, despite the exclusive patent to Coster, and were claiming these as their own work. We will come back to John Fromanteel's service with Coster a little later.

In September 1658 Oliver Cromwell, the Lord Protector, died aged sixty; the very next month, Ahasuerus Fromanteel, now aged fifty-one, made the most important announcement of his life. An advertisement in the *Mercurius Politicus* of 28 October 1658, the issue giving details of Cromwell's funeral, read:

There is lately a way found out for making of clocks that go exact and keep equaller time then any now made without this Regulator examined and proved before his Highness the Lord Protector, by such Doctors whose knowledge and learning is without exception and are not subject to alter by change of weather, as others are, and may be made to go a week, or a month, or a year, with once winding up, as well as those that are wound up every day, and keep time as well; and is very excellent for all House clocks that go either with Springs or Waights: And also Steeple Clocks that are most subject to differ by change of weather. Made by *Ahasuerus Fromanteel*, who made the first that were in *England*: You may have them at his house on the Bankside in *Mosses* Alley, *Southwark*, and at the sign of the Maremaid in *Loathbury*, near *Bartholomew* lane end, *London*.

There is also by the same *Ahasuerus Fromanteel*, Engins made in a new way of his own invention for quenching of fire, which have been thoroughly proved, and found to be effective, whereby those that use them, are not deceived in their expectation; for that they are not subject to choak with Mire, and when they are clogged with Dirt, may be presently cleansed without charge, in half a quarter of an hours time, and

41

fit to work again. Neither are they without extreme violence broken, and by reason of their smalness, may be wrought where there is but little room; and some there be so small, that they may be carried up an ordinary stairs in a house, and there used: And are very serviceable for the washing Vermin off the Trees, and Hops, and for the watering of Gardens, and Cloths, and the like.

There are some very important facts in this announcement which have never been brought out fully. First the journal itself was begun in 1650, running for ten years under the Cromwellian administration. Immediately prior to Charles II's restoration its title was changed to *Mercurius Publicus*. Charles had the publishers discharged and new ones were appointed to run the paper. It lingered for three years only during his enlightened reign. It was a Parliamentarian paper.

Fromanteel himself referred to his new timekeeping aid (the pendulum) as a 'Regulater'. In fact regulator seems to have rapidly become the word used to describe this kind of clock—a regulator clock, or simply a regulator. (Nowadays only a precision clock is called a 'Regulator'.) In 1658 a regulator was *any* clock controlled by the new pendulum. Evidence of the lasting use of this word is found in the 1701 will of Hannah Fromanteel, widow of Ahasuerus's nephew, Murdoch, when she left 'to my kinsman John Fromanteel my Regulator'.

Most important of all in my view is the passage 'examined and proved before his Highness the Lord Protector by such Doctors whose knowledge and learning is without exception'. Fromanteel had shown proof of the pendulum's superiority to Cromwell and his scientific advisors, but when? The period of service which his son, John, served with Coster had only just ended in May, as Cromwell lay dying. Unless we assume that the Protector had a regulator ticking by his death-bed, the examination and proof before his Highness must have taken place earlier. A further claim of Fromanteel's is that he 'made the *first* that were in England', the implication of that phrase being that others had made them in England since. Some of the clocks will run up to a year at one winding—how does one demonstrate a year-clock except by having it running for a year? He also says stocks of clocks are available both at his house and at his son-in-law's at the Mermaid in Lothbury.

What all this indicates is that Fromanteel must have been making pendulum clocks in England considerably earlier than October 1658 because, by that date, he had had time to test his year clocks and prove them before Cromwell and his scientists, and others had already begun to copy and sell the clocks. Furthermore, he had had time to build up stocks of them for sale, and had produced 'fire-engines' as well—yet the earliest known Fromanteel clock bears the date 1658, though the authenticity of this date has been questioned. The dates of Fromanteel's first pendulum clocks are not known. Could the first clock have been made as early as 1655? (We are particularly reminded here of Cromwell's sponsorship of Fromanteel in 1655 for his freedom of London.)

There are other questions that should be asked: for example, could it be possible that Fromanteel was on to the pendulum idea as early as Huygens was, whether independently or through co-operation with the latter? Was it pure coincidence that Huygens published his *Horologium* in September 1658 and Fromanteel published his announcement in October of that very same year, or was it deliberate synchronisation? Had Cromwell's death any bearing on this? Did Fromanteel hasten to publish his announcement fearing that delay might be unwise in view of the uncertain political situation? Restoration of the monarchy would have been anything but convenient for him at this time. Are we to believe that Ahasuerus Fromanteel's entire knowledge of the principle and application of the pendulum to a clock was derived from his untrained son's brief term of service with Coster? Would he, a master of his craft at the age of fifty-one, send his nineteen-year-old apprentice son to learn about a new development which might revolutionise his craft overnight? Such action does not seem to me to be true to the character of the Ahasuerus Fromanteel whose life I have investigated.

We may never know the full sequence of events leading up to the advertisement of 1658, but this date must stand out as a milestone in British horology. Within months the name of Fromanteel must have been recognised as the leading name in the trade, or so we might imagine. And we might justifiably suppose that he basked in honour and prestige during the next year or two—yet no trace seems to survive of any honours from learned circles. The innovation of the pendulum clock was apparently met with stony silence.

But then, these were troubled times. Within eighteen months Charles II was to be restored to the throne. This would surely put matters right with the return of royal patronage in the shape of the king under whose guidance the Royal Society was founded and by whom the office of Royal Clockmaker was restored? This monarch, who is remembered for his encouragement of the spirit of scientific enquiry, would surely reward Fromanteel commensurately with the importance of his work? Fromanteel must now have been first choice for Royal Clockmaker?

Unfortunately not—we might on reflection think it only just that Charles should re-instate his father's faithful servant, David Ramsay, now in very advanced years. As it happened Ramsay died that very summer, leaving the way clear. A petition was submitted for this appointment from one William Partridge; he was hardly in the same class as Fromanteel and the only justification for his applying for the post seems to have been his claim that he was 'bred under Mr. Este' (=East). One can only assume that Charles was advised to choose the master rather than the pupil, and so in November, 1660 Edward East was appointed Chief Clockmaker to the King.

It was in that very month of November 1660 that John Evelyn, the Royalist diarist, had recorded details of a visit to the King's 'closet of rarities' (his collection of rare items including clocks) where he had seen a splendid clock with various sunrise and sunset motions, 'the work of our famous Fromanteel'. Even John Evelyn, who regarded Cromwell as 'the Usurper', was aware of the merit of 'our famous Fromanteel'. This is not the place to digress, but it must be mentioned that this outstanding Fromanteel clock had found its way into the 'closet of rarities' in a very hushed manner. I can find no mention of its purchase in royal accounts under Charles I or II, and the implication is that it found its way there through the interest of the 'usurper' himself, the man who in 1655 saw fit to sponsor Fromanteel for the freedom of the city. Could the clock that Evelyn saw in 1660 have been one of those which Fromanteel claimed in 1658 had been 'examined and proved before his Highness the Lord Protector'?

In 1662 James East was made Clockmaker to the Queen. He was hitherto unheard of, but, examination of Edward East's will, proved in 1696, shows that James was his son so the reason for this appointment seems obvious.

44

David Ramsay's widow was aided to the tune of £600 to help restore her fortunes, plundered under Cromwell. Amid all the in-fighting for royal favours, 'our famous Fromanteel' was never in the running. But the Royal Society, surely here was a body in which he might be recognised? His name never even appears in the Society's records. The man who had done more for English horology than any other was utterly shunned. But worse was to come.

First, we must mention that in April of 1661 Evelyn had paid a visit to Fromanteel's workshop in the company of Christian Huygens. 'I returned by Fromanteel's, the famous clockmaker, to see some pendules.' Evelyn recognised Fromanteel's greatness despite his contrary politics. That Huygens should visit Fromanteel must further show not only a close connection between the two, but indication of where learned sympathies lay. No record exists of Huygens ever visiting Ramsay, the Easts, or William Partridge. It was Fromanteel's workshop in Southwark that was the focus of attention.

In June 1661 Ahasuerus Fromanteel found himself in court, a not unusual situation for him, along with several other residents of the parish of St Saviour's, Southwark. They were charged with breaking the law by subdividing their respective houses into separate dwellings. This was only a minor infringement and I mention it merely to show that Fromanteel still resided in Southwark at this time, no doubt still in Mosses Alley.

Measures were afoot to keep down opponents of the Royalists such as the Anabaptists. Tom Loomes was on the fringes of political activity, and so, probably, was Fromanteel himself. These were difficult times for both their families. The political intrigues which form a background to this story are far too involved to be fully within our grasp. They concern Lieutenant-Colonel Paul Hobson of Newcastle-upon-Tyne and Captain Gower, both former soldiers in the Parliamentary army who had Anabaptist connections in Durham. They were described in 1661 as 'two of the most dangerous fellows in the North' when a warrant was issued for their arrest, they being 'now at Thomas Loomes's in Lothbury'. They were arrested and Hobson spent some years imprisoned in the Tower of London. Thomas Loomes was also arrested but was released again on 17 November 1661 on bond of £1,000 for his 'loyal and peaceable behaviour'. We may imagine who stood surety.

Gower later recounted his story, saying that he was with Paul Hobson when the warrant came to apprehend them both, that he followed the advice of the landlord (ie Tom Loomes) who kept him in an upper room and thence led him into the street, that he went from one friend's house to another, in one of which he continued four months without fire or candle although in winter and only went out at night with his cloak over his face . . . Tom Loomes had given shelter to wanted men and was probably lucky to get off on bond and Fromanteel could hardly have expected royal patronage when his partner and son-in-law harboured the King's enemies.

One accusation against Paul Hobson was that he was acting as an 'agent for a German prince to carry away manufactures'. This suggests a possible connection between Hobson, Loomes, Fromanteel, clocks and Holland—a connection which will arise again later.

It might be as well to summarise here what little else is known of Thomas Loomes. What became of him is something of a mystery. Presumably he worked for his father-in-law, as we know Fromanteel advertised his own clocks for sale at the Mermaid as well as in Mosses Alley. Further, we know of no longcase clocks by Loomes, his only recorded clocks being simple lantern clocks, and only a handful of those seem to have survived, in the tradition of the Mermaid makers *prior* to the Fromanteel connection.

We know that Tom Loomes worked on at the Mermaid, though probably working as a part of the Fromanteel 'factory', until 1664, after which the parish books cease to record his payment of 2d per week rates. A further strange factor suggests that he died in late 1664 or 1665. His last four apprentices, taken between 1660 and 1664, never became freemen of the Company (they were: William Warden, Daniel Worlidge, John White, Samuel Revell). In other words they either left London or died, and my guess is they died. His last apprentice to complete his service was Edward Sedwell, who was freed in October 1664 and died the following August, still in the parish of St Margaret Lothbury, where the Mermaid stood. The year 1665 was, of course, the year of the Great Plague. As the heat of summer reached the highest level within living memory, so did the mortality rate, and by September the death count is said to have reached a thousand a day.

By the autumn of 1665 Ahasuerus's second wife, Sarah, had died. His brother John, the silk merchant, also died aged fifty, appointing Ahasuerus a trustee in his will. Edward Sedwell, one of the Mermaid workmen, died. Tom Loomes and four apprentices disappeared, their bodies probably flung into a plague pit, as the evidence suggests that the Fromanteel workforce and family were struck with the Plague. Those who could, left London and we know that Ahasuerus Fromanteel was among them. We know this because, as we shall see later, he was living in Colchester in 1665 when the Plague spread to that town and he was obliged to leave that place too in great haste. It is doubtful whether many clocks would be made in 1665 or 1666 when the preservation of life and limb and possessions were uppermost in the minds of most Londoners. One in seven is said to have died in the Plague.

The problems which beset Fromanteel at this time were those with which all London clockmakers had to cope. Most no doubt chose to move out of London leaving behind their workshops and such materials as they could not carry with them. However, by midsummer of 1664 Fromanteel had additional problems of a more personal nature. The reader might find it helpful to refer occasionally to the Fromanteel family tree on p 34-5 to understand the various relationships.

After the death of his first wife, Ahasuerus had married again, about 1660, to Sarah Winnock, widow of Samuel Winnock, a cloth dealer in Colchester. Samuel's will of 1658 had provided for his widow and four children with special conditions that in the event of Sarah's re-marrying and dying, any husband was not to get the Winnock monies, which in part at least were to revert to the Winnock children. Any such husband was required to give surety that he would comply with this, but Ahasuerus Fromanteel had refused to do so. John Winnock, brother of Samuel, took him to court in June 1664 for failure to comply.

In October Ahasuerus and Sarah explained to the court that this refusal was based on too high a valuation of the goods left by Samuel, and on the fact that John Winnock had kept for himself certain bonds of Samuel's of over £200 in value, to which he had no right. Furthermore Fromanteel pointed out that he had fed, clothed and educated the four stepchildren, and he wanted the cost of that deducted from any monies he might one day be willing to surrender.

After an interruption caused by the Plague and Sarah's death, John Winnock re-opened the case on 24 May 1666. Three days later the Clockmakers' Company asked Fromanteel to serve as an Assistant—whether their ranks had been thinned by the Plague or whether Fromanteel's merit was beginning to be recognised we do not know. In any event he was too preoccupied at present. He declined and paid £3 to be excused from any future office; he would have nothing to do with them. He presented his side of the court case in June, and typically set out details of how much money he had spent on the stepchildren, not counting their keep: how he had arranged for Sarah to be taught dressmaking; Samuel had been apprenticed to his brother, Murdoch, the silk merchant; Joshua had been taken as his own apprentice ('for which he [Ahasuerus] deserveth to have £20, for [he] has not had less from any apprentice during the last 20 years'); and John had been educated too. Fromanteel also wanted taking into account the interest that had accrued on those bonds that John Winnock held illegally. Altogether something in the region of £600 was involved, a great deal of money then, and this deserved much more urgent attention than the making of a few clocks, which simply had to wait. Nevertheless as a reasonable man and 'for peace sake' Ahasuerus was willing to settle—if his conditions were met.

An interesting sidelight on the Plague is given when Fromanteel explained that he was obliged to sell off many of the Winnock goods cheaply and was forced to leave others behind in Colchester, which 'by reason of the present visitation of the plague there he hath since thought more profitable, convenient and less dangerous to sell than adventure the removal of them to another place'.

In September the Fire of London broke out, interrupting clockmaking and court cases alike. Samuel Pepys watched the fire rage from the safety of Bankside across the river. This, of course, was where Fromanteel lived and no doubt he watched it too as the Mermaid in Lothbury went up in flames. But neither fire nor pestilence could deter John Winnock from his purpose and the case continued with depositions from witnesses taken at the White Hart Inn in Colchester. John had a six-point questionnaire answered by three witnesses. Fromanteel replied with an eleven-point one answered by seven witnesses! Unfortunately, the verdict is not recorded, but I think it may be safe to hazard that Fromanteel won his case.

Time and time again Fromanteel was in trouble, yet each time he had an answer which seemed to have some validity. Were his troubles of his own making or was he really more sinned against than sinning? He was now sixty years old and probably a little weary of constant conflict. He probably scarcely noticed the admission to the ranks of freemen in that year (1667) of Robert Seigniour, a young clockmaker, barely over twenty-one, and he could hardly have recognised in him a future Royal Clockmaker.

Let us consider briefly the disposition at this time of the younger members of the Fromanteel family. Abraham, now aged twenty-one, had been apprenticed to his father in 1662 but had not completed that apprenticeship and had not been admitted as a freeman into the Company. This means he had left London before 1669—quite possibly at the time of the Plague. He might have been shipped out in an empty coalboat returning to Newcastle-upon-Tyne, since we shall see later that he was working there before 1674 and furthermore we know the family had friends or relations there dating at least from Tom Loomes's adventuring days. The youngest son, Daniel, had been apprenticed to his father in 1663, but he too failed to complete that apprenticeship and was never heard of again—perhaps another Plague victim. John Fromanteel was twenty-nine and was probably working in London making clocks, though whether independently or under his father we cannot be sure. Certainly he did make clocks which bore his own Christian name, but at exactly what period is hard to define. Ahasuerus the younger was twenty-seven and working in London as a clockmaker, probably in his father's workshop. Fromanteel clocks at this time are signed (with the exception of John's) as *A. Fromanteel*, although they were probably joint products of father and son. If they had worked separately each would no doubt have wished to ensure the instant recognition of his work by signing it in a distinctive and unambiguous manner.

My view is that at this time Ahasuerus the younger took over the running of his father's business, if only temporarily, for about this time and certainly within the year, Ahasuerus the elder went to the Hague. In mid-1668 Ahasuerus, then in the Hague, authorised Mrs Mary Loomes, widow, of London to receive monies in his name—this was, of course, his daughter. We can only assume that his visit to Holland was for the purpose of setting up a branch of his business. Our knowledge of his life there is scant. (It is known, however, that Abraham was with Ahasuerus in the Hague in 1668.)

We know that in the late winter of 1676 he was back in London because, as usual, he was in trouble. The Clockmakers' Company took him to task for arrears of subscription 'being in arrear of quarterage two and forty shillings [he] pleaded that he should pay only during he being in England (he having bin beyond the sea some years). The Court required him to lay down his full quarterage, and refer himself to the favour of the Court, but he refused to doe it, but paid six shillings in part'. It would seem from the size of the arrears that he had been 'beyond the sea' about ten years, and the 6s he paid would cover eighteen months either at the beginning or end of that period. (Incidentally the Company records distinguish plainly between Ahasuerus the Elder and the Younger, hence there is no danger of confusing one with the other.)

I am advised that no Fromanteel clocks of apparent Dutch construction survive from this time (1666–76), hence we must assume that Ahasuerus's Dutch outlet was for some of the London-made clocks which were exported to Holland. Also we must remember that he was approaching seventy and would be taking things a little more easily than his sons. Probably he was paving the way for future events.

By the date of Fromanteel's return to England (1676) the long pendulum (sometimes called the Royal pendulum) had been introduced. It is not known by whom nor when this took place, except that it was in use by the late 1660s. William Clement and Robert Hooke have variously been put forward as being responsible.

The swing with the older verge escapement was much too wide to allow a long pendulum. The short bob-pendulum, which Fromanteel introduced, continued to be used in bracket clocks and in some lantern clocks even after the Royal pendulum had arrived. This was probably to help with portability in travelling lantern clocks and because both these types of clock with bob-pendulum were less fussy about being absolutely level than when the anchor escapement was used.

Let us complete the story of the Fromanteels and then we can examine some of the reasons for their importance. Our next news of Ahasuerus is in September of 1680 when he recalled his son, Abraham, who had probably worked in Newcastle since he went there about 1668. Abraham returned to London to take up his freedom of the Company on payment of 20s admittance fee. We have no reason to believe that Abraham worked in London prior to 1680. John Fromanteel, Ahasuerus's eldest son, probably went abroad about 1680 and this may be the reason why the ageing father, now seventy-four, called Abraham back to look after the London business. It was about this same year that Ahasuerus the younger went, with his wife, Anna Brown, and seven-year-old daughter, Anna, over to Amsterdam to take over the business there. In July 1692, at the age of eighty-five, the elder Fromanteel made his will, proved in the following spring. He mentioned the three children of his deceased son, John, his daughter Mary, widow of Thomas Loomes, his son, Ahasuerus the younger, his daughter, Elizabeth, wife of his step-son, Joshua Winnock, clockmaker, and of course his son, Abraham. He described himself as sound in mind, but 'antient, weake and crazey in body'.

Ahasuerus the younger had no sons. His daughter married in 1694 in the Hague to Christopher Clarke, another expatriate English clockmaker. Clocks signed *Fromanteel and Clarke* presumably came from this period between 1694 and 1703, when Ahasuerus died. Clocks by Clarke and Dunster are believed to have emerged from a partnership between Christopher Clarke and Roger Dunster from about 1720 to 1730. Christopher Clarke died back in London in 1735, his widow, Anna (Fromanteel), surviving him. Dunster is believed to have died in 1747, for in that year probate of his will was granted to his widow in London.

In England the Fromanteel concern continued under the direction of Abraham, whose occasional brushes with the Clockmakers' Company officials are reminiscent of those of his father. Abraham never married. He lived till the winter of 1730 when he died at the age of eighty-four in New-castle-upon-Tyne, where he had retired. He left his workman, Benjamin Brown, 'a week movement to show the seconds from the centre', ie a clock with centre (or 'sweep') seconds hand, by far the earliest example of a centre-seconds clock so far recorded, though no centre-seconds Fromanteel clocks appear to survive today. With the death of Abraham the Fromanteel family became extinct in the male line, the clockmaking line. There were still descendants through the sons-in-law and stepchildren (the Winnocks and Primes), but Ahasuerus the father and his three sons were alone responsible for the Fromanteel clock empire. Male Fromanteels survived in other branches of the family, but they were not clockmakers.

Why were Ahasuerus Fromanteel and his sons so important? Simply because they set the pattern. Ahasuerus did first what others later might
embellish, modify, improve, but the nature of the longcase clock, which
Fromanteel introduced in 1658, set the pattern for the next two centuries.
Thomas Tompion has been called the 'father' of English clockmaking, yet
when Tompion became a freeman of the Clockmakers' Company, Fromanteel was ready for retiring. If we wish to see clockmakers in terms of ances-
tral figures, then we could call Fromanteel the 'grandfather' of the English
'grandfather'!

Of course there were other famous makers during Fromanteel's lifetime,
men like Robert Seigniour, William Clement, Daniel Quare, Henry Jones,
David Ramsay, Joseph Knibb, all of them top names, yet their contribution
was insignificant alongside that of the Fromanteels. Let me just quote one
item—it comes from John Aubrey's *Brief Lives and other Selected Writings*
edited by A Powell, published in 1949:

> 'Mr. Nicholas Mercator made [= had made?] and presented to King
> Charles the 2nd a clock ('twas of a foote diameter) which shewed the
> inequality of the sunn's motion from the apparent motion, which the
> King did understand by his informations, and did commend it, but he
> never had a penny of him for it. Well! This curious clock was neglect-
> ed, and somebody of the court happened to become master of it, who
> understood it not; he sold it to Mr. Knib, a watchmaker, who did not
> understand it neither, who sold it to Mr. Fromantle (that made it) for
> £5, who askes now (1683) for it £200.'

Who were the Knibbs? Samuel Knibb, free of the Clockmakers' Company in 1663, is known only through three surviving clocks, which are so
similar to Fromanteel clocks that it is thought that Knibb worked with him
or copied from him. Samuel was probably dead by 1683, which leaves his
cousin, Joseph, who went to London in 1670. Many fine clocks by Joseph
survive. In 1675 Sir Richard Legh of Lyme Hall, Cheshire, bought one from
Joseph Knibb in an ebony case at £24, having decided against a walnut one
at £19. What was this clock which Knibb could make no sense of and for

which Fromanteel could ask £200? Could it even be the one described earlier by John Evelyn with sunrise and sunset motions? We do not know, but
the story of it would seem to put the two makers into perspective.

Only one man was a near-equal to Fromanteel and that was Edward East,
who was born four years before him and survived for four years after him to
the amazing age of ninety-five. East was a freeman of the Goldsmiths' Company as early as 1627. We know that East and Fromanteel worked together,
though perhaps for a very short spell. East had the ability, the patronage and
the glory. But it was Fromanteel and his pendulum that showed the way; it
was Fromanteel who made 'the first that were in England'.

CHAPTER 3
PROVINCIAL BEGINNINGS

As has been shown in the foregoing chapter, Fromanteel was the originator of the longcase clock, and it was this type above all others that was to become *the* British clock. Before his introduction of the pendulum in 1658 there were virtually no domestic brass clocks made in the provinces; so the Fromanteel story is an essential preliminary to the story of country clock-making. There were, of course, a very few lantern clocks, with balance-wheel regulation, made in the provinces at an earlier date, but the reader is unlikely ever to see one. Bernard Mason, in his book *Clock and Watchmaking in Colchester*, dates the earliest surviving lantern clock made there as being about 1645. One survives by Robert Harvey of Oxford from the early years of that century. At this early time, however, the provinces did not offer a very wide market for domestic clocks, hence those who wished to specialise in that craft and improve their expertise tended to drift to London, just as Fromanteel had done, for there there was an abundance not only of highly skilled masters but of the customers for the product.

Lantern clocks with balance-wheel regulation were not too accurate, and, with variance in timekeeping by as much as a quarter of an hour a day, they needed frequent resetting by checking with a sundial. Consequently virtually all of these were wound daily, some early ones twice a day even. Fromanteel's pendulum changed this overnight. Its greater accuracy now made it worthwhile to increase the length of run from one winding—a week, a month, three months, even a year. But Fromanteel's longer dur-ation movements needed heavier driving weights. Hence the long wooden case was devised as supporter and container for these, and with the intro-

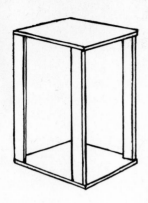 

The post-framed or 'birdcage' construction, shown on the left, developed from the old lantern clock. The plate-framed construction, shown on the right, was used for the longcase clock from its very beginnings

duction of this case, the clock moved for the first time into the sphere of furnishing items.

Lantern clocks had been made on a four-posted constructional frame, like a four-poster bed with upright corner posts and flat plates at the top and bottom (p 20). Fromanteel's new clocks were constructed in a different manner with upright plates front and back between which were held the wheel train pinions, the whole 'works' held together by short horizontal corner posts, called pillars. This was a stronger construction altogether, as was needed by the much heavier weights these clocks had to carry, especially if of long duration. All these changes involved in the switch between relatively primitive lantern clock and the more sophisticated plate-framed clock came as a direct result of the contribution of Ahasuerus Fromanteel with the pendulum. Others copied, but he did these things *first*.

Now let us just re-cap for a moment. Before 1658 we had a very small lantern clock industry in the provinces with a more productive centre in London (and to a certain extent in Edinburgh too) and fringe areas, spreading out ever more thinly with increasing distance from London. Anyone who tries to locate a pre-1658 (or even post-1658) lantern clock made in

Yorkshire, Lancashire, or indeed any northern county, will see how very thinly they were spread there. The counties closest around London felt the London lantern clock influence more strongly. Once Fromanteel's pendulum-controlled, plate-frame clocks arrived, the provincial interest increased. There was now more point in owning a clock if it kept reasonable time. Northern clockmaking, and indeed all provincial clockmaking, now began in more earnest. However, the very strong influence of London as the centre of lantern clock production had far-reaching effects, which were felt in two distinct ways.

The lantern clock continued to be made in London and the south not only after the introduction in 1658 of the pendulum, but even after the arrival of the long pendulum about ten years later; and this despite the fact that the lantern clock with long pendulum (and anchor escapement), was a none too practical affair. The lantern clock underwent *modification* in design by adapting it to the new Royal pendulum, and in this form it continued to be made in London and the south for over half a century more. Because the long pendulum was not designed for the lantern clock, its introduction to it was not altogether happy; the uncovered weights and pendulum were subject to much outside interference (the perfect plaything for a cat), and the long pendulum meant that the clock had to be fixed to the wall in a more precise manner.

The lantern clock had never been a very popular form in the north. Hence, when the provincial areas of the north really got under way with domestic clock production, there was not the same lantern clock tradition to which the northern makers might adapt these new pendulum ideas. Therefore domestic clockmaking in the northern provinces began at once with the true pendulum clock, that is the plate-construction longcase clock. Here we seem to have the root cause of the relative scarcity of the lantern clock in the north compared to the south, where because of its long tradition it flourished even after it had outlived its real relevance.

A further difference between northern and southern methods seems to stem from this root cause. The southern lantern clock with its four-posted construction gradually gave way to the more sensible 30-hour longcase form (more sensible because its weight-lines and pendulum were protected by the case), but this southern 30-hour longcase clock was built along the

56

four-posted constructional principles of the old lantern movement. This was known as a posted-framed movement, sometimes called a birdcage movement, and this type of movement is very largely, though not entirely, confined to the south. In the north the 30-hour longcase began, virtually from its conception, as a plated clock and a northern 'birdcage' movement is very uncommon.

The diagrams on page 55 show these distinct constructional differences. The 8-day clock, and those of longer duration, were always built on the stronger plate-frame principle.

The general absence in the north of the lantern clock (and of the birdcage 30-hour longcase) does not mean there are not a few examples and by briefly considering these, we are led a little further into the beginnings of serious provincial clockmaking. We have already seen indications of the pattern we may expect from the disposition and dispersion of the Fromanteel family. With the maturity of Ahasuerus Fromanteel's family coinciding with the maturity of the longcase clock, we can almost foresee what was bound to happen. The old pattern of an almost total concentration in London began to change. In London the competition became fiercer as the numbers of clockmakers increased more rapidly than the market. The enormous potential market in the provinces proved too tempting to remain unexploited. Young Abraham Fromanteel went off to Newcastle-upon-Tyne; Ahasuerus the Younger went to Holland; brother-in-law, Andrew Prime, and his son went to Norwich; stepson Joshua Winnock moved to Colchester . . .

The Fromanteel pattern of family members taking the trade into the provinces was repeated in a great many clockmaking houses as other London-trained apprentices also took their skills away from the capital after training. Some provincial clockmaking traditions therefore quite literally had their origins in London.

The most interesting examples of this may be seen in counties far removed from London, as in the northern counties. It is significant that of the few clockmakers in this area by whom lantern clocks *are* known, a good proportion had an immediate London origin. Abraham Fromanteel of New-castle-upon-Tyne made lantern clocks. So did Thomas Cruttenden of York, formerly an apprentice of John Fromanteel, who moved to York in

1679 less than two years after completing his London training. In Westmorland, however, where there was virtually no influence at all from London, I cannot trace a single record of a lantern clock. In Lancashire too, with precious little London influence, lantern clocks are very scarce. Further south counties such as Suffolk, Norfolk, Essex, and even more distant ones like Devon, Cornwall, Somerset, Oxford—in all these areas the lantern clock was more popular, and in my view this was because the London contact was more pronounced there. London had particularly strong clockmaking links with Bristol, Bath, Exeter, Oxford, Colchester and Norwich; much weaker were those with Yorkshire, Westmorland and Lancashire (although very strong *watch*making connections were maintained with the latter county).

Now that we know some of the influences on early provincial clockmaking, let us consider the nature of those earliest clocks. The lantern clock continued in production in the south, Midlands and East Anglia, very much in the form it had taken in London, though two basic types were made. Most were now made with the new and more accurate long pendulum. Some, however, were still made with the old short (or bob) pendulum, which was a less accurate timekeeper. Why make clocks with a less-than-satisfactory type of pendulum, when the more accurate long pendulum control was now known to all clockmakers? This was not done out of ignorance. It was done for convenience on small portable lantern clocks used by travellers and often fitted with alarmwork. These travelling alarm clocks fitted neatly into a small wooden carrying box, which the traveller could conveniently take with him when journeying away from home. At night he could hang the clock from any convenient bacon hook on the bedroom wall, and thus the short pendulum offered convenience both in portability and in setting up the clock, since it was more tolerant of imprecise hanging. These smaller travelling alarms are less common than the normal long pendulum versions. Bracket clocks also retained the earlier verge escapement (with short pendulum of course), on account of their being carried from room to room and therefore needing to be less fussy about being set down level.

This London pattern of the lantern clock continued in the south as described, though it gradually gave way to the longcase clock, but there was one important difference which we must consider with regard to all provincial work. The difference was that of quality. The provincial maker by and large had to keep his price down to the absolute minimum to ensure himself a market, and this meant that he was not free to produce spectacular lantern clocks with a superabundance of engraving and even the occasional use of solid silver, such as were sometimes made by men like East and Fromanteel. In 1656 when the Reverend Giles Moore, rector of Horsted Keynes, Sussex, bought a clock from Edward Barrett of Lewes, he paid £2 10s for it. We know that this must have been a balance-wheel lantern clock, as Fromanteel had not yet brought in the pendulum. We also know that for the next century or so an average provincial lantern clock could still be bought for £2 10s (two-and-a-half weeks' wages to our well-to-do shopkeeper). But one would not have been able to buy a lantern clock of Fromanteel or East calibre for such a small sum (£100 in today's values).

Before any experienced collectors begin to throw up their hands in horror, let me hasten to add that I am not for one minute suggesting that provincial makers were never capable of making superb lantern clocks; some of them, of course, were. The Knibbs of Oxford were a very special case because of their London connections; so was Cruttenden of York for the same reason. Even so, not many provincial lantern clocks can compare in splendour with the best London ones, not so much because their makers lacked the ability, as because they lacked wealthy customers.

We have seen that the lantern clock was the ordinary man's clock. Despite some magnificent examples having been made for the aristocracy, the ordinary lantern clock was the cheapest clock on the market. With provincial clockmaking beginning to build up momentum by the last quarter of the seventeenth century, the 30-hour longcase clock rapidly began to take over as the dominant form. Such contemporary prices as we can trace show that the lantern clock was maybe a shilling or two dearer than the 30-hour longcase *movement*, but the additional cost of a case for the latter made the total cost quite a bit more. The wooden case in its simplest form could be bought in pine or oak from as little as 10s to £1, but nevertheless this was an *extra* on the cost of a lantern clock.

A handyman, of course, always had the option of knocking up a case for himself, and some undoubtedly did so. I have seen cases which were apparently made in this way, being nothing more than a straight-up-and-down protective box-cum-stand, serving the basic needs of the clock but having no shape or 'style' of any sort, and evidently made by a man who was not familiar with the normal case shape. I know of three such cases, all late seventeenth-century and apparently contemporary with the clocks they contain. One houses a clock by no less a person than Edward East, presented by him to Queens' College, Cambridge in 1664, yet the case is no more than a box—this one, however, is believed to have been re-cased later in the seventeenth century, but it still bears out my point. Let us not forget that the important bit was the clock—the case was nothing more than a supporter and container for it, and any 'stylistic' aspects of the case are for show and for no other purpose.

Since there can be no doubt that the 30-hour longcase clock was better suited for its purpose than the lantern had been, it has always seemed very odd to me that the authors of some older reference books, who praised the 30-hour lantern clock, also went out of their way to decry the 30-hour longcase form as a cheaper and degenerate type of clock. This can only have been out of ignorance of the fact that, rather than being cheaper, it was in fact more costly than the lantern. As to 'degenerate', the 30-hour plated movement was designed as such from its inception, whilst it was the lantern clock, designed originally for balance-wheel control, which degenerated by being adapted first to the short, and then to the long pendulum, neither of which was ever designed for it! But then our concern is to follow the development of clocks, rather than to attempt to understand mistaken conceptions of that development.

Occasionally, one comes across hybrid forms such as lantern clocks fixed into long cases or sometimes just into hanging hoods to keep the dust out. There were also lantern movements which had square longcase dials fitted, and even arched dials. These hybrids, however, were just partial solutions, not really effective substitutes for the optimum 30-hour form, which was the plate-framed clock in a true long case.

So far we have mentioned only 30-hour clocks, the cheapest form which had the widest market. Eight-day clocks were also made in the provinces from the same time. These were always of plate construction and they were a considerably more expensive proposition. The 8-day clock was almost twice as costly as the 30-hour type, hence it appealed to the wealthier customer. Because of this the 8-day clock tended to be made more by town and city makers, where it might even account for the bulk of their output. An 8-day clock was so unusual an item for some countryside makers that an order for one was almost an event in itself.

If the 8-day clock was more unusual on account of its higher cost, the spring-driven table clock, usually called a bracket clock, was even more costly. It started from about twice the price of the 8-day longcase type. Hence, whilst London makers may have excelled in bracket clocks, in provincial work they formed only a very small proportion of the total picture. Even among city clockmakers it is unusual for as many as half a dozen examples to be recorded by any one provincial maker. In country districts there are whole areas (Westmorland for instance), where barely a single example has been recorded, and most country makers probably never even attempted to make them. This was probably because the very high proportionate cost put them outside the price range of their customers, and not, as is sometimes suggested, because provincial makers could not get the springs. Of course they could get the springs, just as a provincial maker could get any other clock parts which he wanted to buy-in rather than make for himself. Apart from the larger London suppliers or makers there were also specialist part-makers in the provinces, even springmakers, as early as the later seventeenth century.

A ratio of prices of clocks of equal quality shows us clearly the relationship between the various types. When Christian Huygens made his first pendulum clocks for sale, his prices were (in the Dutch currency of 1659):

Thirty-hour weight-driven, striking	80 [guilders?]
Eight-day weight-driven striking	130 [guilders?]

Suggestions that a clockmaker more than twenty miles from London did not have readily available parts or tools or casemakers, just do not stand up to examination. By the end of the century the London position was such that a considerable number of makers, even those with very famous names, might opt to buy-in stock parts such as spandrels, wheels or wheel-blanks, rather than spend their valuable time in making mundane parts. Cases would be ordered from the casemaker, engraving sent out to specialist engravers to the trade, and the master would then be left free to devote his time, talents and inventiveness to designing and planning, rather than to working with a file. From the very inception of the Clockmakers' Company we can clearly see that some members specialised, for instance, in engraving work or casemaking (for watches), and the implication is that enough work of this specialised sort was farmed out by clockmakers to supply them with that living, even in those early times.

Let us be quite clear then that just as these specialist part-makers had existed in London from almost the beginning of the century, by the later seventeenth century makers in the provinces also had available adequate supplies of tools, materials, parts and specialist services such as engravers. The extent to which provincial makers made use of these services is another question altogether, which we shall examine shortly.

By mid-century Lancashire was the major producing centre of clock and watch tools, of which the file, in many varied forms, was the most important. Wheel-cutting machines, called 'engines', were always used for roughing-out wheels, the teeth then being cleaned up by hand filing. The machine did the measuring, spacing and cutting, and every clockmaker, even the most humble, had a wheel-cutting engine, which was usually his most costly and precious piece of equipment. The total worldly possessions of Thomas Bridge, clockmaker, of Bolton, Lancashire, assessed on his death in 1717/18, amounted to £17 6s 6d, of which his tools and materials totalléd almost £14. A poor man therefore had a far greater proportion of his capital invested in equipment than a wealthier one, as there was a minimum stock of tools which any clockmaker was obliged to keep. Bridge's tools were

	£	s	d
two pair of balows [bellows]		8	0
One stedy [steady] and two stokes [stocks]		19	0
fore hamers [four hammers]		4	0
five pair of forgeing tongs and nail twol [nailmaking tool]		2	0
iron belonging two ould church clocks		4	0
the grett lath [large lathe] and sandbox and flasks		3	6
a weigh beam			6

two turn benches and two pair of hand vices	11	0
files and scrue plates [screwmaking plates] and other work twoles [tools]	2 10	0
one lath [lathe]	15	0
the Ingen [wheel-cutting engine]	4 0	0
one second hand clock	1 5	0
two grindlestones [grindstones] and frames and the barell Ingen [barrel-cutting engine?]	3	0

From this inventory we can see that Thomas Bridge, a maker typical of hundreds of other near-anonymous provincial makers, cast his own brass, (re-)forged his own steel, cut his own wheels, made his own screws and nails and probably did his own engraving (hence grindstones for sharpening engraving tools). If he wished he could have bought all these items ready made, as his more famous London contemporaries such as Tompion almost certainly did. Why did he not buy them in? Not because he was an expert brassfounder, wheelcutter, screwmaker and engraver all rolled into one; though he doubtless became very skilful at all of these processes. He did it purely because it was *cheaper* to do it himself than to pay others for their services. Price was the major factor, and it was essential for him to keep his clocks down to a price which his local customers could afford.

Several implications follow from this state of affairs, the most important one being that the work of a provincial clockmaker (at this time) tends to reflect far more truly the skill and craftsmanship of that man, than does the work of a famous London maker. This does not make the product better; on the contrary it would almost certainly be inferior in quality of execution than the combined efforts of several top London component makers. It does, however, make it a more personal product and therefore more interesting, because each one-man-band provincial maker tended to have his own idiosyncratic ways of doing things. Each man was a 'school' of his own. Because of this, provincial clocks offer a most interesting and enlightening field of study, and one which is all the more exciting because the sources lie virtually untapped. Hardly anyone has yet bothered to look in detail at the most individualistic and fascinating areas of clockmaking—the provinces. A whole series of new and important aspects await discovery.

Let me quote one example. There was a fashion, perhaps mostly in the northern counties, and mostly in the late eighteenth century, to design clocks with concentric hands, so that instead of the normal hour and minute hands radiating from the centre of the dial, these clocks also incorporated a long seconds hand and a calendar hand in the centre, in other words *four* hands radiating from the same point. For various reasons, it was not a very satisfactory system. It worked, but generally the result was not worth the technical complexities involved, and in use they were often more trouble than a conventionally laid-out clock. If you are able to turn up a reference in a text book to this type of clock, you might learn that this method of centre-seconds hand began in the period 1740–70 and yet, as was mentioned in the last chapter, Abraham Fromanteel left a will in 1731, in which he bequeathed 'a week movement to show the seconds from the centre' to his journeyman, Benjamin Brown. This implies that this type of clock had been in production probably as early as 1710.

Another type of clock appears to have been made in the northern provinces during the seventeenth and early eighteenth centuries, though I know of no surviving example. That was the household wooden clock— presumably a clock made with wooden wheels along the lines of those made in Germany and America in the nineteenth century (and earlier).

In 1675, Sir Thomas Wentworth of Bretton Hall (Yorkshire) died, leaving in his inventory 'in the hall one brass clock—£2'. In 1667 William Richardson of North Brierly (Yorkshire) left 'in the hall Roome—one brasse clock—£3'. Both these must have been brass lantern clocks, though neither need have been of local make. Richardson's father, Richard Richardson, who had died in 1656, had apparently left a wooden clock—'a wood clocke—13s 5d', and since from its date and value it could not have been a wooden-*cased* clock, it would seem that we have a household clock made of wood. Unfortunately, this still does not help us to build up a picture of this unusual timepiece.

More extraordinary still is an item in the inventory of Thomas Bridge of Bolton:

'Three pans, one wood Clock, one wood watch 15s 0d'

This puzzling statement I can only explain by suggesting that the 'clock' was a normal striking one and the 'watch' a non-striker, since the word 'watch' was used in the seventeenth century to refer to the 'going' train as distinct from the striking train. Both do seem to have been made of wood, just as the famous Yorkshire-born John Harrison made wooden-wheeled clocks in the days before he found his fame in London. What is surprising is the incredibly low valuation of these devices, although since other inventories list similar articles at similar prices, it is obviously not an isolated or freakish valuation. In contrast, goods made of brass, even household vessels such as pans, were always valued seriously, since brass was very valuable if only for its scrap metal worth. In 1700 brass, even at scrap value, was worth not less than 9d per lb and was considerably more valuable than pewter.

A brass clock, even of simple lantern variety, was very often one of the most costly single items in a household, even in a well-to-do household. In addition to the wooden clock William Richardson's will mentions a £3 brass clock (notice that 'brass clock' seems to have been the contemporary term for 'lantern clock'), and it ranks among the highest-valued single items, alongside 'one bed with furniture' at £5. Sir Thomas Wentworth's £2 brass clock can be compared alongside almost a whole armoury of: '7 cases of holstered pistols, 1 pare of holsters without pistols, 10 muskets, a sword, 2 holberd, two battering axes, 4 drums and five suits of armour and the horse collars', which altogether amounted to just over £15 . . . in other words a brass clock was apparently equal in worth to one suit of armour, one pair of pistols, one drum, one sword and two muskets! The inventory of Joseph Pryor of Liverpool, watchmaker, shows that his 'clock and case' at £4 10s (eight-day longcase clock?) was by far the most costly item he possessed, the next nearest being his 'desk-and-bookcase' (bureau-bookcase?) at £2 5s. Mere guns were very low in comparison: a 'long gun', for example, was worth 7s 6d, a 'musquet' 4s, a 'small fowling piece' 4s and a 'carbine' a mere 3s 6d. The inventory of Jonathan Woolfenden of Rochdale in 1715 showed his clock at £1 15s (30-hour longcase?) as his costliest possession except for his bed. George Taylor's 1722 Liverpool inventory also has his clock and case (8-day longcase?) as being worth more than anything except for his bed.

I mention these few comparisons simply to help us get house clocks into

65

their appropriate position in the general range of furniture items. The very different emphasis that we place in our present-day values of antique items tends to obscure the fact that the clock, even if a modest 30-hour one, was usually the most important and costly piece of furniture in the home.

By 1747, the *Universal Magazine* tells us, the clock had 'become the genteelest Piece of Furniture in almost every cottage'. The son of a mid-nineteenth century Welsh clockseller wrote: 'When I was a lad my father had in his shop nothing but large eight-day clocks . . . When a young couple were married, in particular a farmer's son or labourer, his ambition was to buy one of these clocks as *the principal piece of furniture* for the house, and scores of them are to be found up and down the countryside'. (In the nineteenth century the 8-day clock was much more common than in the eighteenth.)

This knowledge must colour our attitudes when we consider the relative positions of 8-day and 30-hour clocks and why it was such a vital struggle for so many rural clockmakers to keep their products within the financial reach of their clientele.

Whilst early provincial clocks would tend to be mostly the less costly 30-hour types, there were naturally some makers, predominantly in the larger towns, who produced 8-day ones. Eight-day clocks of fine quality are, however, exceptional before 1700, and even before 1750, after which the city makers had a larger clientele with the taste and funds for better quality 8-day clocks.

There is no doubt that, where they had a customer willing to pay for the extra work involved, many provincial makers could turn out clocks of superb quality. It is amusing to find authors who explain away the occasional occurrence of a superb clock by a provincial maker by assuming that it was bought from London and merely had the local retailer's name engraved on it. This mistaken belief, which presupposes that anything of 'quality' must have originated in London, is tinged with irony when we begin to discover that, in some respects at least, provincial makers were suppliers to the capital—for instance, with clock and watch tools, and particularly watch parts.

Clocks of superb quality survive by John Williamson of Leeds, Jonas Barber the younger of Winster, Henry Hindley of York, Thomas Lister the younger of Halifax, the Cockey family of Warminster, Deodatus Threlkeld of Newcastle-upon-Tyne, Richard Comber of Lewes, Thomas Moore of Ipswich, Thomas Ogden of Halifax, the Barker and Coates families of Wigan, the Finneys of Liverpool, John Benson of Whitehaven, and many many others. It does not by any means follow that all clocks bearing these names are fine quality ones, as it all depended on what the customer was willing to pay for.

As an illustration of this, Isaac Simpson of Chorley, Lancashire, received an order, in 1822, for a clock through his cousin, William Fell of Slaidburn, who acted as agent. 'I received an order for one 30-hours clock . . . as handsome a face as you can make it, and make it a good one for they wholly depend on my word, and send it as soon as you can. You will receive the money when they receive the clock, which will be £2 16s od.' You did not get a masterpiece for £2 16s od!

Having first considered some of the background conditions in which provincial clockmaking began, we may now begin to look a little more closely at the clocks themselves. We have considered the basic types involved—lantern, bracket, longcase, 8-day, 30-hour. We know the relative importance of one to the other, both in actual monetary values and in the relative quantities we may expect to meet with. We also know in what parts of the country, whether town or village, we may expect to trace varying types. It is most important that we form a clear picture of this from the outset, because a type which is rare in one area may have been commonplace in another.

It is also essential that we recognise that London, though important for being the place where British clockmaking originated, very soon ceased to influence provincial work. The old-fashioned concept, that later provincial work is to be judged by the degree by which it resembles London work of an earlier, or even contemporary, period, is quite misleading. Different as they might be from each other, there was a stronger common link between the 30-hour grandfather clock in a Cornish tin-miner's cottage and the pompous mahogany musical clock in a Lancashire industrialist's townhouse, than existed between any of these and London. London had played its part, and hereafter the provincial clockmakers went very much their own separate ways.

CHAPTER 4
THE NUMBERS MEN

Some clockmakers numbered their clocks and these form a very special group, which I call the numbers men. They are special simply because by numbering their clocks they have left us a superbly clear trail to follow, a set of fingerprints of vital importance in the detective work of horological research.

The numbers enable us to draw many interesting conclusions rather than hazard guesses: to recognise unmistakably the chronological order in which a man's clocks were made; to ascertain how many clocks a man made; to help recognise a genuine clock from a faked one by its agreement in style with the period suggested by the number; to analyse and study the output of a maker by breaking down the ratio of 8-day to 30-hour clocks and the proportion of bracket, lantern or turret clocks to come from his workshop. Best of all is the fact that most of these numbers men were unimportant provincial clockmakers, whose clocks may still be met with in abundance, thereby offering every enthusiast an equal opportunity of seeing, studying and recording them. The numbering of watches was a far more common practice, and watch serial numbers usually form a different sequence to those of clocks by the same maker.

George Goodall of Aberford, Yorkshire, was born in 1731 and died in 1796; clocks of his survive with numbers from 98 to 578. Thomas Crofts of Halton, near Leeds, worked in the 1750s and some numbered clocks are recorded by him which are dated too. Such a dated and numbered clock is a very helpful example, as one can soon begin to calculate a man's yearly output, and eventually establish the year of manufacture from the number.

It was not only the makers of brass dial clocks who numbered them. Richard Blakeborough, who worked in Yorkshire' numbered all his painted dial clocks. They have his number painted after his name: Blakeborough, Otley, No 2343. Did he really make (or sell) so many? I cannot say for certain, but it seems quite possible.

The above were Yorkshire makers from my own back yard and I mention them because I happen to be familiar with their clocks. Others did the same thing in different counties, using either a number, a date, or both. For example, we know of John Bell of Hexham, Northumberland (no 153) and John Ayrey of Hexham, Northumberland (no 965), both of whom worked in the late eighteenth century, as did Samuel Wainwright of Northampton (nos 2,826, 3,063). Thomas Hampson of Wrexham, Denbighshire, died in 1755 and clocks of his survive numbered between 16 and 1,563.

It has sometimes been doubted that insignificant provincial clockmakers really did produce such large numbers of clocks as some of the higher serial numbers imply. Such doubters suggest that a number such as 1,563 of Thomas Hampson was reached because he started at 1,000 or 1,500. Those of us who study the subject hold different views, as we can see from the occurrence of clocks numbered at regular intervals.

While many put their numbers plainly on the dial, there were others who numbered their clocks in a less obvious way, for example on the movement plates, where the number would be hidden to all except restorers who dismantled the clock, or to the very keen enthusiast who would deliberately search for such numbers. Jonas Barber the younger of Winster, Westmorland, did this, as did his journeyman and successor, Henry Philipson of Winster and later of Ulverstone, Lancashire. I know of clocks by Barber running from 101 (c1746) to 1,435 (c1797), and by Philipson from 1,444 (c1802) to 1,613 (c1812). The latter claimed to have reached 1,670. Some clocks by Lawrie of Carlisle are numbered on the frontplate and are hidden from general view (see plate on p 178).

The enthusiast who wishes to look into his local numbers man needs to record details (ideally photographically) of dials and movements by that maker, study them with a magnifying glass, and set out the results in sequence on analysis paper. Much that is surprising will probably appear; in addition to the sorts of conclusions that I mentioned earlier, the seeker may

Thirty-hour clock by Jonas Barber the younger of Winster, c1764 (no 683)

learn from the regular occurrence of small stylistic features whether the maker did his own engraving or sent engraved work out to a specialist, whether he bought all his painted dials from the same source, how his dial styles developed, the sorts of hand patterns he favoured, whether his case-work follows any pattern and so on.

My local numbers man was Will Snow of Padside, near Pateley Bridge in Yorkshire, who lived only a couple of miles away from my own home, and lots of his clocks survive in the district, signed for instance as *Will Snows 660* (see p 72). He did not bother to put the place on the dial, perhaps because he sometimes took them to Otley market to sell, perhaps because few people knew where Padside was anyway. Will Snow was born in 1736 and died in 1795 on his farm, for he was a farmer as well, just as many of these country clockmakers were. I have seen many of Will's clocks, and all those I have seen were brass dial, 30-hour ones. Some painted dial ones do exist by

70

Oak case of Barber clock, c1764

Thirty-hour clock by Will Snow, c1775 (no 660)

Will Snow, but these are probably by his son, William the younger. I suppose he must have made some 8-day ones, but I have yet to come across one. They range numerically from 30 to 923, not a bad output for a man who was a part-timer.

There was nothing special about Will Snow. He is merely representative of thousands of lesser provincial makers of his time. Like a great many country makers he had a secondary occupation, no doubt as a precaution against leaner times. The town makers often did the same thing in so far as they had sales shops where they could branch out into barometers, thermometers, silverware, jewellery, cutlery, hardware and all manner of kindred goods. The country maker could not do this, and so his secondary income was often from farming, innkeeping, smithing, carpentry, or associated country crafts. Some country makers had more unusual sources of income. Evan James of Dolgellau (working 1759) was also a harp-maker. Jacob Littlemoor of Ruabon was also a potter, till he went bankrupt in 1728. Henry Jones of Llandysul (1819–80) was a baptist minister and poet as well as a self-taught travelling clock repairer. Walton Alderson of Leyburn, Yorkshire was a schoolmaster in the early nineteenth century, as was James Airey of Grasmere, Westmorland; the latter is said to have dressed clocks in the classroom during lessons! James Barber of York (died 1857) was a stagecoach proprietor. Frederick Frank Dobson of Driffield, working 1817–58, made clocks as well as being postmaster, brass-founder and fishing-tackle dealer. William Bracewell of Scarborough, working 1834–58, was also licensed to let horses. The variety is amazing.

However, because of Will Snow's numbering system we are able to pin down the periods of his stylistic development. The earliest of his clocks that I know (no 30) is dated AD 1758. This was a two-handed 30-hour clock, unfortunately now converted to 8-day duration by virtue of having been fitted with a totally different 8-day movement. Luckily, I was fortunate enough to be able to purchase the rejected 30-hour movement and this was my very first experience of the Mark One Will Snow movement. Engraved behind the calendar wheel was the legend:

> *This piece of work it may be seen*
> *When in my grave I long have been*

Of course, the sentiment was true enough, though no doubt if he knew of the movement now attached to his dial he would turn in his grave! The illustration (p 74) shows the unusual layout of a Mark One Will Snow movement. The very primitive appearance, which is indicative of his own individual style, was responsible for leading the Dutch dealer, who bought the dial-less movement from me, to suppose that it was a seventeenth-century one, regardless of the fact that I explained to him its local origin! Such a movement layout is unique to Will Snow's early clocks and is proof that such a maker of simple country clocks thought for himself and made his own parts and castings, without having recourse to buying-in ready-made parts from trade suppliers.

73

William Snow 30-hour movement, Mark One, seen from the back. Apart from the primitive appearance, the shaped and cut-out plates make it almost a cross between a 'birdcage' and a plate movement, although it is strictly a plate one. Made about 1760

His dials also display interesting evidence of the extent of his own skill. His chapter rings show an engraving craftsmanship which is competent enough. These were almost certainly sent out for engraving by skilled commercial engravers, of which he would have had a reasonable choice—men such as Edward Moore of Leeds, who advertised in 1741 'I engrave plate, etc . . . likewise engrave, lacker and silver Clock Faces at the lowest prices . . . ' (interesting evidence that these dials were sold with a silvered coating, and not as bare polished brass). John Butterworth of Leeds advertised in 1759 'engraver in the Bull & Bell Yard in Briggate, engraves all sorts of bills, clock faces, etc' and Sylvester Forrest of Leeds advertised in 1770 as 'seal-cutter and copperplate printer—clock faces engraved and finished'. There were always skilled engravers available, like Charles Blakeway of All-brighton, Warwickshire, who in the late eighteenth century offered: 'Dyal plates engraved at 2s 6d each; wheels cut for clockmakers at 6d per set'.

What is so interesting about Will Snow's dials, however, is that, like the dials of many country clockmakers, the chapter rings show a quality of engraving which is considerably superior to that in the engraved dial centre. This is presumably indication that Will engraved his own dial sheet centres, but sent out the chapter rings to a specialist. If one looks closely at one of his engraved dial centres one can often see evidence that the dotted outline of the design was pricked out first in guide lines to be followed by the smooth flow of the engraving tool, but that the engraving sometimes runs off or misses the dots. With a skilled engraver this would not have happened, and indeed marking-out dots or lines should not show. Will knew what to do, but could not do it as expertly as a specialist engraver such as Edward Moore. Despite this, for the sake of economy, he was willing to accept his own inferior engraving of the dial centre.

That he was not a skilled engraver is not a criticism of Will Snow in particular, as it applied to very many provincial clockmakers, even (perhaps especially) to those of high repute, where in the past a misunderstanding of the situation has caused writers to credit some clockmakers with superb skills which in reality they never possessed. One such is Thomas Lister the younger of Halifax, who has a deservedly high reputation for fine clocks including complicated world time dials—yet he could not engrave! As evidence of this, we find that one of his clocks is signed *Thomas Liston, Halifax*, although his name was, of course, Lister, not Liston. This suggests that he did not engrave it himself, but sent it out to a specialist engraver who misread his copy.

Errors of this sort are not particularly uncommon. A clock exists signed *Thomas Redford, Leeds* in error for Thomas Radford. I was recently shown another Thomas Radford clock, where the lettering was engraved in a scrollwork design in the dial centre and the word *Leeds* was upside down! The engraver constantly turned the plate round when working, and in allowing his concentration to lapse had not noticed his error till it was too late.

These errors and slips tell us a little more about provincial clockmaking, in so far as no modern manufacturer would allow goods to leave his premises with such blatant imperfections. These would be spotted by quality

William Snow 30-hour movement, Mark Two, seen from the back. Still highly individual in style, the cut-away plates are now simplified. Re-using the cut-away brass parts and employing steel for the pillars and cock resulted in considerable cost reduction. Made about 1780

controllers. That the famous Thomas Lister would permit a clock to be sold with his name misspelled rather than scrap that dial and start afresh, is one more indication of the importance of the cost factor. Error or not, it had to do. Sometimes, one finds, when removing a chapter ring for cleaning, that the engraver has started to work on the reverse side, and, having made a bad slip, he has turned the ring over and begun anew on the other side. When one occasionally sees engraved odds and ends, even doodles, inside the plates of movements, it is often obvious that these engraving attempts are very feeble in comparison to the polished work on the dial—further evidence that the clockmaker himself was seldom capable of good engraving.

In sidetracking on the topic of engraving errors I have not abandoned Will Snow, as one of his clocks, which I had, presented further evidence of this 'make-do' attitude. Will Snow's clock no 658 was a 30-hour two-hander with unquestionably original (and unaltered) Will Snow (Mark Two) movement of the 1770s. Yet it had a single-hand type of chapter ring, marked out in quarter-hour units! I can think of only one explanation for this—that he was temporarily out of stock of two-handed chapter rings and, rather than wait for his next delivery, he went ahead and made do with ring no 658, which he had already in stock. It is only fair that we draw attention to such shortcomings where they exist in provincial work. It is difficult to imagine a top-flight London maker's willingness to accept inadequacies of this sort.

I mentioned Will Snow's Mark Two movement, and the illustration represents the layout of one of these, differing most obviously from the Mark One in having more simply shaped plates. It is important to consider why Will Snow's plates took this most unusual 'skeleton' form. Skeleton plates are extremely unusual in English clocks, so unusual that Will Snow's plate pattern may even be unique, although I understand that skeleton plates are not uncommon on American longcase movements of the late eighteenth century. Before anyone suggests that Will Snow was an American, I will explain why I think he used this form, and this is probably also why it was used in America.

It was for economy. Brass was costly, even more costly than pewter, and, even at second-hand scrap value, brass was worth 10d per lb weight in the early eighteenth century. By casting his plates with only just sufficient brass area to accept in position and strength the wheel arbors and other vital fastening locations, Will may have saved considerable weight of brass. By using steel for the cock and pillars (again most unusual English practice) he made further brass savings—steel being only one-tenth of the value of brass. His dialplates also had cut-out holes (see illustration), as was often the practice with northern makers, where the cut-out areas would be hidden behind the chapter ring. There may well have been additional benefits in the casting processes in using the skeleton layout—perhaps fewer blow-holes in the brass, so often found in early solid plates. There may have been other benefits in having a cut-out type of dialplate; it would be less likely to distort and buckle if being worked with a frosting punch to produce a matted centre. The castings were probably done in this pierced form.

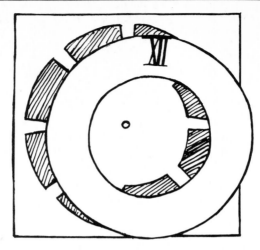

Dial showing the chapter ring pushed aside from the dialplate to reveal cut-away sections (shaded) characteristic of many north country clocks

The major saving might amount to $1\frac{1}{2}$ lb weight of brass, which in those times was equivalent to half a day's wages. Whether this meant an extra shilling in Will's pocket or the ability to reduce his retail price by one shilling and thereby undercut the prices of other local makers, we cannot say. But Will Snow's practical application of common-sense economies must have been of considerable benefit to his volume of trade, and incidentally serves today as a most helpful aid to our study of the numbers men and their methods.

Let us now glance at a clockmaker in a remote region in Wales. Samuel Roberts of Llanfair-Caereinion is a very good example of a humble country clockmaker-cum-farmer. He is at the very lowest end of the scale in so far as his clocks are the simplest and cheapest type of the period. This is not intended as a critical comment on the quality of his workmanship. He simply supplied what his customers wanted.

Whilst he *may* have been capable of superb work, it is unlikely that he was, simply because an apprentice-trained full-timer spending all his working hours at clockmaking must on average develop skills superior to those of a man who taught himself and made only one clock a month, which was the case with Roberts. Roberts made his clocks in a country area where money was spent only grudgingly on such luxuries—consequently his products must represent the very humblest of British provincial clockmaking. But it is important that we do not feel it is beneath us to study his clocks because of their humble station in the hierarchy.

Sam Roberts was to the Montgomeryshire farming folk what Ramsay and East were to kings. An appreciation of his manner of working is every bit as important to our understanding of British clocks as is a knowledge of the top handful of Londoners—it is possibly more important, for you will come across more 'Sam Roberts' clocks than you will Fromanteels. One might spend a lifetime without ever coming across a Fromanteel, but one meets with clocks of the Roberts type in every second antique shop in Britain.

Roberts has left a unique record in his own numerical register of clocks he made. The conclusions we can draw from an examination of his notebook apply to a whole strata of clocks throughout the country, though we recognise that Roberts is an extreme example. The little notebook contains entries starting in 1755 and finishing in 1774, and is a complete record of every single clock Roberts made during that period. As he numbered each clock he made, this notebook was his record of serial numbers against each of which he briefly described the type of clock, for whom it was made, and the price, with occasionally other additional details. Here is a random early entry:

> John Pugh of Cancappan
> his clock was made and finnish'd
> April 30th 1757 Numbered 122
> Prize £2-5-0. ye Body 78, 72, 36, Dial
> 48 by 13 by me Sam Roberts.

The numbers refer to body wheel, dial wheel, etc and denote the number of teeth per wheel. Occasionally he also mentions the pendulum length, which varied according to the layout of the wheels. Sam was constantly experimenting with wheel and pendulum sizes, the latter ranging from a length of 2ft 5in to 3ft 10in.

Insignificant as it first may seem, this little notebook is extremely important as it is one of very few such records that survive, and the only one I know of that can be seen to be comprehensive. The numbering system enables us to be sure that it is a record of *all* the clocks that Sam made in that time. The numbers start at 102 (8 August 1755) and end at 396 (15 April 1774) with a gap between 113 and 121 where a page is missing. As very many country clockmakers were men like Roberts, the conclusions to be drawn about rural clockmaking are far reaching.

Llanfair-Caereinion is about ten miles east of Welshpool. That Roberts could draw customers from as far as almost thirty miles away to the north, west and south, and from forty-five miles away (the coast) to the east, must indicate more the lack of much local competition rather than any special talents of this maker, since the very simplicity of his clocks shows that no great strain was put upon such talents as he had. This may become more evident when we analyse the type of clocks he made. His customers came not only from his own county of Montgomeryshire, but from the adjacent counties of Merioneth, Denbighshire and Radnorshire.

The entry of each customer's name in the book, apart from adding a certain general interest by way of pedigree for a present-day owner of such a clock, indicates something very important, something which is not generally realised. Every single clock he made on this list (288 clocks) was *made to order*, made for a particular person and to the specifications of that customer. This contradicts the more usual view of rural clockmaking, which has been to assume that the clockmaker made the clock and then found a customer who would buy it. Hence, we can see clearly that the restricting influence on rural clockmakers was quite definitely from the demands of the customer, who for the most part wanted a cheap functional item, not a work of mechanical art.

What kind of clocks did Roberts make? All the ones listed had brass dials, which in itself is interesting. As we shall see elsewhere, the painted dial was already being advertised as a regular trade item by 1772, but in mid-1774 Roberts was either still unaware of this or had decided to carry on with his brass dials as usual.

Virtually all his clocks were 30-hour ones, only six clocks in twenty years being 8-day ones, which rather strangely he calls 9-day clocks. One (no 154) was a month-clock, actually a 5-week clock. One seems to have been a turret clock (tower clock). He calls it a *large* clock, but its price indicates that it was something quite out of the ordinary, not simply a larger-than-average case clock. One of his 8-day ones was a three-train, three-bell, quarter-chiming clock, a 'ting-tang' chimer we would probably call it today. Such a clock strikes the hour on one bell, as is normal, but has two additional bells, which strike the three quarter hours: one 'ting-tang' at quarter-past, two at half-past, three at quarter-to and four on the hour. His largest call was for single-handed 30-hour clocks, but it is interesting to see the proportions gradually change: in 1755 only about one-sixth of his yearly output was in two-handers, by the end of the period (1774) this proportion had increased to as much as one third of his output.

Surprising features were available as optional extras, surprising in the sense that the customer seems to have preferred the basic single-hander with an 'optional extra', rather than pay almost the same price for the basic two-hander. Roberts distinguishes a two-hander by calling it one 'with ye minuitts on it'—a one-hander, of course, showed quarter-hour divisions, not minutes. The nature of the 'optional extras' can be seen from a study of his price-structure, aided by such notes as Roberts thought fit to put down. First we must understand that there was not the sort of inflation in those days that is so familiar to us today. Sam's prices remain unchanged in twenty years! His basic clock was a square brass dial 30-hour one-hander, which he sold for £2 5s. When we remember that the 30-hour lantern clock of 1656 had cost £2 10s, we realise that prices seem to have been pretty stable for over a century. In practice he must have had to trim his prices occasionally for a customer who drove a hard bargain or conversely he stuck on the extra shilling, where he knew he could get away with it, for his prices reflect the occasional variance by as much as two shillings either way. For £2 10s one could have the more 'up-to-date' two-handed version, an 'extra' which cost 5s 0d.

Another 5s extra bought a repeater, which would seem to deserve an explanation. Some books will tell you that repeating work on longcase clocks is very unusual. This is not so; it was quite common. Those books will also tell you that it is superfluous, as repeating work was useful only when it was dark, otherwise one could see the time on the clock and would have no need to repeat the last hour. The conclusions drawn are that repeating work was useful on a bracket clock, which might very well be used in a bedroom. As longcase clocks were not (usually) bedroom clocks, authors have been unable to see the purpose of repeating work on them. However, Sam Roberts and his customers seem to disagree with these authors and repeating was apparently important enough to induce some customers, who could not afford the two-handed clock (or could not read it), to pay the extra 5s for a one-hander *with* repeat work, than for a two-hander without. Quite a number of Roberts' clocks are specifically mentioned as being repeaters. I have seen numerous clocks by all sorts of provincial makers which also had repeating

Thirty-hour clock by I P—Asby c1755

work, and I can say from my own experience that they are far from rare. We would be better advised to ask ourselves *why* this was required rather than to conclude that it ought *not* to have been required.

On an 8-day clock repeating work was normally nothing more than an extra steel spring rod about 6in in length with a hole in its protruding end through which one could tie a cord. The cord could hang down passing through a hole in the seatboard into the interior of the trunk. Alternatively it could pass through a hole in the hood side or in the moulding below the hood, and in these latter cases might run over a small pulley attached to the woodwork (see p 82).

On a 30-hour clock it also entailed this steel spring and further, its presence dictated the use of rack striking rather than the cheaper locking-wheel striking system employed on the normal 30-hour clock. (A 'repeater spring' on a clock with locking-wheel striking is not for repeating at all, but is for re-adjusting the clock in the event of its having wandered out of striking sequence, as it might do if for example it were allowed to run down completely.)

Each time the cord of a repeater is pulled, it will strike out the last hour, from a minute or two after that hour until perhaps ten minutes to the next hour. During the period of ten minutes to the hour and that hour it may either refuse to repeat or repeat the *approaching* hour, owing to complications caused by the clock's preparing to strike. It is therefore 'accurate' in repeating for fifty out of the sixty minutes of each hour. If the strikework is assembled imprecisely after cleaning or repairing, then the precision of the repeat may become less accurate.

For those who have experience of the technicalities of clocks, I should add the following note. Some repeating work is designed with a separately mounted snail controlled by a star-wheel, and this type of more costly repeating work is even more 'accurate', as it may repeat the last hour to within perhaps four minutes of the approaching hour (see p 168). However, normal strikework does the job almost as well if the snail is cut and set with precision.

The repeating work to which I refer is controlled by a spring-loaded trigger arm, and it can be recognised by the presence of that arm, for this fulfils no other function. Sometimes, indeed frequently, one sees a hole in the end of the lifting-piece of a non-repeating clock. If a string were tied to this lifting-piece end, then that in a sense could make the clock 'repeat', but it would be inaccurate, causing it to repeat the last hour till about half-past, after which it would repeat the approaching hour. A string tied to the lifting-piece end in this way is *not* proper repeat work, which must have the spring arm in order to ensure the return of the lifting-piece to its proper position after repeating.

We are forced to recognise that repeating work was desired by many customers, but why? How and when was it needed? We do not know for sure, but we can feel reasonably sure that the original owner did not, in darkness, make his way to the clock with the aid of a candle or lamp and pull the repeater cord to find out the hour, when he would have been able to see the time on the dial. Several explanations are possible, but that one is certainly not. We might just find it credible that an uneducated person, or a child even, might be unable to tell the time on a clock dial, but could count the number of strokes on the bell if the repeater cord was pulled. Such people would always be in a minority after 1750, and by 1800 and later almost everyone would be able to tell the time from the dial, yet one *does* find repeaters on post-1800 longcase clocks.

My explanation requires us to picture the gloomy half-light in a household just stirring in the early morning, with the woman of the house or servant girl downstairs early and busy at her first tasks of the day, such as lighting the fire or making the breakfast. The rest of the household including the master, about whom most things revolved, is still in bed, half-awake. The servant girl in passing the clock in the hallway gives the repeater cord a pull—thereby announcing to those not yet out of bed that it was already after 6, 7 or 8 o'clock as the case may be. If it produces no response, she pulls the cord again a few minutes later. In other words the clock is being used as a kind of repeating reminder to the master of the house that he had better get moving, a sort of intermittent alarm.

Repeaters, as I have explained, have the cord either inside or outside the case. Some, however, have no cord and show no signs of ever having had one, on clocks which do have this purpose-built repeater spring. Why? A 'wrong' case could be one explanation, but I have seen quite a number where the repeater has never been used and we cannot assume that all had

had their cases changed later. Furthermore, I know some clocks with unused repeater springs which are *known* to be in their original cases. We can only assume in these instances that whilst the clockmaker fitted the repeater spring, the customer decided he did not need it and never bothered to use it. This might apply where the extra spring-arm was the only extra piece fitted, its cost being negligible, but it would not apply where, for instance, rack striking was purposely fitted at an extra cost to the customer of 5s, as with Samuel Roberts' 30-hour repeaters.

Another optional extra was mentioned for the first time on clock 302 (11 July 1769). It cost 3s extra to have a chain drive, which he mentioned there-

Thirty-hour clock by Sam Roberts, Llanvair, made in 1767 (no 265)

after in his specifications each time it was required. The implication is that his earlier clocks had all been rope driven. The price difference was not just because the actual driving rope was cheaper than chain, but because more work was entailed in filing the pulleys to take the chain links, whereas rope pulleys were plain. I do not suggest that chain drive was unknown before 1769; it looks very much as if Sam had preferred rope simply to keep the price down.

Eight-day clocks, of course, did not run on rope or chain but on 'catgut', which, I am told, was actually made from the intestines of sheep rather than cats. The only early reference to this substance, that I know of, appears in Sam Roberts's notebook, where in 1761 he made a note about payment for a pair of 'Bowell Lines'. For those sufficiently interested, the recipe for converting sheep intestines to clock lines is given by Mr E. J. Tyler in *The Craft of the Clockmaker*.

An important aspect of Sam's prices is that in every instance the price was for the clock and clock alone. Clock cases are never mentioned in his book and he seems never to have involved himself with cases. The customer must have made his own arrangements for a case, though probably Sam knew a local carpenter to whom he would refer enquiries. We can be quite certain that clocks selling at £2 5s to £2 10s, as most of his did, were sold caseless. Cheap as cases then were, even a softwood one would add at least another 15s or £1 to the bill. The illustration (p 85) shows Roberts's clock no 265; the entry reads:

> Ezekel Thomas of
> Llanbrynmair his clock was
> finished 30th Augst 1767
> numbered 265 prize
> £2-14-0 by me Saml. Roberts

This was probably £2 10s for the two-handed version, 5s extra for the repeater, less 1s discount. His rare 8-day clocks appear to have cost £4. His three-bell quarter-chiming ting-tang clock, also of course an 8-day one, cost £6 6s. The one turret clock cost £9 10s. On one occasion he made a dial only for Margaret Morris—presumably she had a clock with a damaged dial. The price of this is not clearly legible, though it looks like 12s. Sam was, however, prone to normal human failings and in error he gave two clocks the same number, no 156 for Mr Evans, being followed by no 156 for Mr Griffiths. Hence we see that the normal rules of logic do not always apply to clocks, and it is possible for two different clocks to exist, each having the same number, and yet each being genuine!

Sam obviously took in other clocks for repair, and some of these were evidently of a superior type to his own. In 1761 he noted details of 'Mr Wheeler's clock'—whether Wheeler was the owner or maker we do not know. That this was not a clock of his own making is evident from the fact that he does not number it. In 1765 he jots down details of 'Barker's clock'—again no number indicates that he did not make it. Neither Barker nor Wheeler appear as names of his purchasers. Wheeler's clock had a moon dial in the arch, and presumably this was so unusual to Sam that he thought it worthwhile measuring the various parts of dial and moonwork, perhaps for his own future use. His clocks were probably all square dial ones.

In 1760 an interesting repair job came along—Mr Williams's clock was to be 'turned to long pendulum'. This was presumably a short pendulum lantern (or longcase) clock, probably dating from many years earlier, needing conversion.

On 30 January 1772 a most interesting footnote on clock 348 adds, 'the first in ye club'. Here and there amongst his normal clocks he keeps noting another for 'the club', till eventually in December 1773 he notes 'last for ye club', being the twenty-second clock noted in this way. This is the earliest example I know of a clock club. Before we examine just what a clock club was, we should continue with our brief look at Sam's output.

Over the years his production had gradually increased from about a dozen clocks a year, rising to around twenty, his busiest year being 1769, when he turned out twenty-two clocks. Then in 1771 business fell off drastically—he produced just thirteen. Could it be just coincidence that this was about the time when the new painted dial came out, and was Sam, persisting with his brass dials, losing business to customers who went elsewhere for the new type of dial? We will never know. However, with trade this bad, Sam had to do something to bring the orders in. He could hardly lower his prices, which were already at rock bottom.

He decided to try to boost trade by forming a clock club and it had the desired effect, for, over the two years during which the club functioned, his output rose to twenty-three and twenty-two in 1772 and 1773 respectively. Sam Roberts was probably not the first to form such a club. Most likely he was adopting a known trade practice. What happened was as follows.

The clockmaker got together, probably in the local tavern (what was good enough for the Clockmakers' Company was no doubt good enough for Sam!) a group of customers, who agreed to meet once a month and each pay a subscription. The sum produced at each meeting had to be enough to pay for a clock. If a clock price was 50s, then one had to have fifty members each paying a shilling, or twenty-five each paying 2s, and so on. In one month 50s was paid in, one clock was made, one club member got a clock— perhaps lots were drawn to decide who got the clock. The first 'purchaser' had of course paid only one subscription, and the difficulty was that the other members must each ensure that he continued to pay his monthly dues. Each month another 50s was raised and another customer got his clock. The main benefit for the clockmaker was that he could sell clocks to those less well-off, who perhaps might never raise 50s in a lump sum, but who could manage the monthly subscriptions. It was a form of hire-purchase. Sam's club had twenty-two members, each meeting once a month and each paying 2s. The last member got his clock almost two years after paying his first subscription.

The late J. K. Bellchambers, in his book *Somerset Clockmakers*, published in full the list of rules of a clock and watch club run by T. Stocker of Martock. The sum was to be £4 4s for a watch, or if a clock and case were desired instead, then the receiving member was to pay an extra £1 1s on delivery. The rules allowed for various penalties for a member who failed to pay up. Each clock was to be guaranteed for seven years; each watch for one year. The club was begun in 1808. This is the only clock club known to me other than that run by Sam Roberts. We should note the considerably higher price Stocker charged for his clocks which *included* cases.

Another country clockmaker left notebooks as evidence of the way he did business, this one from the far south of the country—John Belling of Bodmin, Cornwall. There were four generations of this clockmaking family, all named John, but it was the eldest one who kept the notebooks

88

during the years 1737–54 and later. His notebooks, now owned by a descendant, seem to consist of all manner of business and personal jottings, not purely of clock matters, and it is unlikely that the clocks mentioned are in any way comprehensive. Some of the details in the books are quoted by H. Miles Brown in his interesting book, *Cornish Clocks and Clockmakers*.

John Belling's notebooks appear to confirm what we have already discussed with regard to country makers, namely that they made clocks mostly to order. He notes the details required on the clocks such as dial size, 30-hour or 8-day, etc. Like Sam Roberts he offered both two-handers and one-handers in his 30-hour range, which made up the bulk of his output. Like Roberts, he distinguished them as 'a playne 30 howar clock' (ie one-hander) or 'a 30 howar clock with howar and minut' (ie a two-hander). Where a calendar was also required he called it a 'day of the month clock'. His clocks were, of course, in the southern tradition of post-framed construction.

Belling probably cast his own spandrels, sometimes using tin, which was probably more readily available than brass, and perhaps cheaper too. On occasions Belling took scrap metals, the essential ingredients for his craft, in part payment for his clocks, the very same practice we have already noted amongst northern makers. One notebook entry concerns the making of three pulley wheels for a roasting jack. Others relate to such varied personal items as setting two rows of hangadown beans (= runner beans?) and hiding smuggled brandy in a cupboard and are interesting in that they tell us the sort of man Belling was. He was not, of course, a numbers man, and might therefore seem out of place in this chapter, but his notebooks form such a rare type of record that he must be mentioned alongside Sam Roberts, as affording us valuable information about country clockmakers, their lives and their art.

CHAPTER 5
STYLES

As the eighteenth century progressed, the ratio between 30-hour clocks and 8-day models changed, slowly at first, but with ever-increasing momentum. Yet 8-day clocks, while becoming increasingly popular, tended to remain with the town makers, and it is probably true that for the rural clockmaker the 30-hour clock was always his main product, right to the end of the century, and even beyond.

Why do I bother to stress this breakdown and distribution? Simply because today we are lazy and have too often in the past been led to believe that the daily winding of a 30-hour clock is a nuisance, and that we ought to consider seriously only 8-day ones. Those who wish to hold this view are, of course, entitled to it, so long as they realise that if they seek a provincial clock of 1700 and insist on an 8-day one, they will search for a long time. Bringing forward their stipulated period to 1750 will ease the search, but not until the 1770s was the proportion of 8-day clocks high enough to make a modern collector's search for one a relatively straightforward affair. By this time the painted dial had arrived and the brass dial rapidly began to lose favour.

In looking briefly at the stylistic development of clock dials, we shall consider initially those with brass dials, and we must constantly remind ourselves that what applies to an 8-day clock may not apply to a 30-hour one, even of the same date. Provincial longcase clock dials at the opening of the eighteenth century would tend to be small, 9–10in square, gradually increasing in size and reaching 11in by mid-century, even 12in by the 1770s. Dial size alone usually gives a good indication of the date. A 12in dial in

Thirty-hour clock by Johannes Shepley, c1710

1700 or a 9in one in 1770, for instance, would be almost an impossibility. Early dials were square; those with an arched top began about 1720–30. Since arched dials were more costly to make and to case, it follows that arched dials are more frequently found at this time on 8-day than on 30-hour clocks.

The plate shows a typical 30-hour dial of about 1700. The heavily engraved centre, perhaps in a sense a carry-over from lantern clock days, is typical, but would not be so on an 8-day clock. This particular clock by John Shepley is a one-hander, which is also typical of this period. Latinisation of the maker's name as *Johannes Shepley* is in itself usually an early sign and was unusual after about 1720; sometimes the word 'fecit' is added to the

Month-clock by John Williamson, Leeds, c1695

Latinised name. A two-handed clock was not impossible at this time, but a one-hander was more usual until mid-century. Single-handers lingered on until about 1780 in the north, later still in some conservative southern areas, such as East Anglia. An engraved-centre dial of this sort might be met with from about 1690 to 1725 on a 30-hour clock.

The 8-day dial centre was usually a more austere affair at this time, more dignified and plain, as can be seen in the plate above. The biggest difference in appearance is in the dial centre, which is 'matted' or 'frosted', that is, roughened all over to give a non-reflecting, sandpaper type of finish,

Marquetry case of Williamson clock,
c1695

Eight-day clock by John Smallwood, Chelford, c1700

intended as an aid to clarity with the *two* hands. The presence of two hands dictated that they must stand out clearly so that each of them could be distinguished. On a one-hander all that mattered was the position of the hand; with the two-hander one had to read not only the position of each, but also had to be able to tell clearly which hand was which. An 8-day clock was practically never a one-hander (actually one example is known). At this period the 8-day dial centre sometimes had ringing around the winding holes (see plate on p 93), and usually a little engraving around the calendar aperture, but was otherwise very plain and formal.

94

Eight-day clock by John Burges, Wigan, c1725

Oak and walnut case of Burges clock,
c1725

On both 8-day and 30-hour clocks the calendar, if present, would normally show through a square box above the VI (occasionally a circular hole
was used instead). By about 1760 the square date box became a semi-circular
'lunette' and after about 1775 this often gave way to a calendar pointer (see
plate on p 168 although this is an unusually early example).

The arched dial was introduced about 1720–30 and at first was mostly
used for the more costly 8-day clocks, being especially useful if any extra
feature was desired such as moonwork to show the moon's phases and lunar
date. The square dial still persisted on most 30-hour clocks and on many 8-
day ones, especially if it was important to keep down the total clock height.

Sometimes a clock is seen where a separate arched portion is added to the
basic square dial sheet (see plates) instead of being cast in the same single
piece of brass. This occasionally happened where a clockmaker was willing
to 'make do' with his normal stock of square dials for all his clocks, simply
adding the arch in those few instances where he needed to; this meant he
needed to carry a stock of only one type of dial sheet. Often this happened
in the early years of the arched dial (1720–40), when clockmakers were not
yet using sufficient quantities of the new arched design to make it worthwhile making special arched castings. Sometimes, however, an added arch
is a sign that a square dial has been made into an arched one later (maybe to
make the clock fit a different case) and one is well advised to look closely at
an added arch.

Decorations, called spandrels, were normally used to fill the four corners
of the square dial, and often the two sides of an arch. These were brass castings, filed up and chased before being fitted (by means of a screw). A clockmaker could, if he wished, buy these in from trade suppliers. Even a man
who insisted on casting his own spandrels, would normally use a design currently popular, and therefore most spandrels one sees fall into quite a small
range of popular designs—perhaps twenty to twenty-five designs would
account for those on almost every clock one sees. We will discuss the development of spandrel design in detail a little later.

Sometimes a provincial clockmaker would decide against using spandrels, maybe to keep down the quantity of costly brass used. Instead he
might leave the corners entirely empty, though this is unusual. More frequently he might use an engraved design for the corners: sometimes a

97

Thirty-hour clock by William Porthouse, Penrith, c1735

simple pattern of engraved circles, sometimes engraved flower-like decorations, sometimes an engraved verse. A popular corner verse used by a handful of north country makers in the early eighteenth century runs (in each corner respectively): *Behold this hand; Observe the motion's tip; Man's precious hours; Away like these do slip.*

98

By about 1730 the engraved centre of the 30-hour clock had given way to a frosted finish, like that of its grander 8-day colleague. Superficially therefore the 8-day and 30-hour dials now looked quite similar. This may well have been the intention of the makers of 30-hour clocks in copying the 8-day matting technique, as this superficial similarity was played on to an even greater degree by some makers, especially in Lancashire and Yorkshire. They often made the 30-hour so like the 8-day in appearance that the differences would be apparent only to someone opening the case door or examining the movement. They gave the dial winding holes, and sometimes even winding squares, just like the 8-day clock had. Of course these squares were no more than dummies, purely for appearance's sake, and one still wound the clock by pulling the internal rope or chain. The idea behind this mild deception was that visitors to the house would be fooled into thinking that the owner had the costly 8-day type of clock, when in fact he had not. Sometimes winding holes were engraved into the design and not actually pierced through.

Eight-day clocks normally had a seconds dial below the XII numeral; 30-hour clocks did not. An 8-day clock without one is a little unusual; a 30-hour clock with one is very unusual. There are several reasons, not least being that some 30-hour clocks have pendulums which do not beat a true second. However, if a 30-hour clock were fitted with seconds dial, the seconds hand would run anti-clockwise because of the wheel train layout. This would look a little comic, though I have seen clocks with anti-clockwise-running seconds hands on occasions.

Sometimes, however, a 30-hour clock was given an extra train of wheels in order to reverse the direction and allow a clockwise-running seconds dial to be included on the dial. This was an unusual practice, but it seems to occur most frequently on 30-hour clocks with dummy winding squares and presumably it was done to increase the resemblance to 8-day, in allowing the normal 8-day seconds dial to be fitted. The seconds dial usually had a miniature chapter ring of its own. Each second was normally marked out on the *inner* edge of this band and numbered 5, 10, 15, etc in the earlier period, pre-1740 say. Later the seconds markings moved to the *outer* edge of the seconds ring and the numbering frequently ran 10, 20, 30, etc. This can help as a dating guide, but it is by no means a hard and fast rule.

One-handed clocks, such as that in the plate on p 91 had markings between the hour numerals to register quarter-hour units, and these quarter-hour markers were set along the inner edge of the chapter ring. Chapter
rings of one-handed clocks remain relatively unchanged over the years.
Chapter rings of two-handed clocks, however, change considerably and
can assist in identification of period.

The chapter ring of a two-handed clock was basically just like that of a
one-hander *plus* the minutes (we are reminded that Sam Roberts actually
described two-handed clocks by that very feature, 'one with ye minnuits
on'). By the opening of the eighteenth century minute markings were set
outside the engraved minute band. The two-hander still kept the quarter-hour markings of the one-hander on the inner edge of its chapter ring,
and also kept its large half-hour indicators, often a kind of fleur-de-lis. The
reason for the retention of the inner chapter ring markings was probably so
that those unaccustomed to two-handers could, if they wished, still read the
clock as a one-hander by ignoring the minute hand and reading the hour
hand position along this inner band of quarter-hour markings. Early two-
handed dials, then, were dual-purpose and some also gave an extra read-
ing-point in that they marked the *half-quarter* units (see p 95). The device by
which it was marked was often an asterisk, diamond or crucifix symbol positioned between the minute numbers at each $7\frac{1}{2}$ minute point that was not
already marked by a minute number. For instance the marking might run 5,
symbol, 10, 15, 20, symbol, 25, 30, and so on. The half-quarter marker
gradually disappeared from use as familiarity with the 'new-fangled'
minute divisions spread, so that it seldom appears after about 1730–40 and
hence is a useful feature in helping to date an early clock.

In the seventeenth century there is evidence that the half quarter of an
hour was the smallest time unit in popular use. We have already come
across evidence of this in Chapter 2. When Ahasuerus Fromanteel advertised his 'fire-engines' in 1658 he pointed out with pride that in the unlikely
event of their becoming clogged with dirt they could be cleaned in a few
minutes, but he did not say that, or few would have understood what he
meant. Instead he said that they 'may be presently cleansed without charge
in *half a quarter* of an hour's time'. This was the smallest unit of time readily
understood at that time. Fromanteel marked the half-quarter units on some

Carved datestone set into the house of John Spencer, clockmaker, of Birchenlee Farm, near Colne, Lancashire, showing a single-handed clock dial. The initials stand for John and Sara Spencer

of his own clocks by a dot, and was probably the first clockmaker in England to mark half-quarters.

The gradual decline of the one-handed clock reflected the increasing education of the population as the century progressed. The changing style of the two-handed chapter ring also reflects this same increasing sophistication and therefore can help us in dating a clock. By about 1750 the quarter-hour units on the inner edge of a two-handed chapter ring began to be omitted (see p 102), though for a while yet the half-hour marker remained. By about 1760–70 the half-hour marker too was dropped. This tended to happen a little earlier with 8-day dials than with 30-hour ones, since the former catered in general for a slightly more sophisticated customer in whom more education might be assumed.

Interesting evidences of the continuing popularity of the one-handed clock amongst country folk may be seen in Sam Roberts's output. When John Spencer, the clockmaker/farmer, built his house at Birchenlee, Lancashire, he carved the year '1760' into the datestone and also incorporated a

Eight-day clock by James Park, Kilmalcolm, c1760

carved clock dial—a single-hander, another indication that his average customer recognised a clock by its one-handed rather than two-handed appearance.

In mid-century a short-lived fashion arose for what is known as a 'Dutch' minute band. This was a wavy minute band (see plate above) and was more commonly used on elaborate arched dial 8-day clocks with painted moonwork in the arch than on simple clocks. On such clocks the seconds dial is often recessed into the main dial sheet and its border is often scalloped to match the wavy minute band (see p 102). The 'Dutch' minute band occurs mostly in the 1750s and 1760s.

The matted dial centre took a new turn in the ten years before 1765; there was a return to engraving. The small engraved area around the date box (on a matted background of course) began to spread about 1750 and ultimately covered most of the dial centre, so that one had a heavily engraved dial centre with matting as a background. The next step was the omission of the matting and the engraving now stood out more boldly against the polished brass surface. In the south there was perhaps a slower changeover to engraved centres, and sometimes no changeover at all.

All engraving on a clock dial was filled with wax to enforce its clarity. This was normally black wax, but decoration was sometimes waxed in red as an attractive variation. An engraved area was then silvered over with chloride of silver paste. Any engraved information therefore stood out clearly in black (or red) against a silvered background (unengraved parts of the dial were naturally left as polished brass). Silvering could only be done when the background surface was plain, so that for instance there could be no silvering on a dial centre where matting was used as a background to engraving. Today many dials have had all their silver polished away and therefore present an all-brass appearance quite different from that intended when the clock was made. What happened was that once the lacquer coating over the silver began to deteriorate (it would hardly last more than fifty years at most), the silver itself began to turn black with exposure to the atmosphere. Houseproud owners have frequently taken to polishing with metal polishes or abrasives, which rather than restore the silver simply would remove any that was left, rubbing the dial down to bare brass.

Skilful restorers can resilver today by traditional methods, and this is well worth the cost. Of course one must never try to polish a dial that has been newly resilvered for reasons just explained. To purists who dislike the idea of having a dial resilvered and prefer to keep it in 'original' condition I would point out that there is nothing 'original' about dirt. Resilvering can be likened to reupholstering chairs. If the covering on eighteenth-century dining chairs were worn to shreds the owner would have the choice of re-upholstering or sitting on the stuffing. Cleaning a brass dial with metal polish to make it shine, is exactly the same as tearing the torn covering off the chairs to leave the stuffing showing. Owners who like to see a brass dial polished to show a shiny brass surface are entitled to hold that view, but they must understand that they are changing the appearance of the clock from what was intended by its maker.

About 1770 the engraved double band marking the minutes gave way on some clocks, especially 30-hour ones, to dotted minute markers (see p 72). This was almost certainly done as a time-saver and for cheapness, as it would be quicker to buzz dots onto the ring with a drill than to engrave two concentric circles and divide off each minute. Dotted minutes were probably copied by makers of brass dials from those found on the earliest painted dials of the 1770s. We shall see other evidence which suggests an attempt at copying from painted dials. About 1775 we find the first attempts at this, a brass dial made from one sheet of metal. Instead of having a separate chapter ring, seconds ring and spandrels, all the necessary information and decoration was engraved onto that one sheet. We call it a one-piece brass dial, and a well-engraved one can look very fine.

Such a dial was completely silvered all over. It is highly likely that the one-piece silvered dial began as an attempt at copying in brass the new style and new legibility of the painted (white) dial, which was introduced in the early 1770s. One-piece engraved dials were far more popular in the south than in the north of England, though one does find them in Scotland. In northern England this type of dial was seldom used except on clocks with circular dials, including regulators. In southern England and in Scotland it survived into the early years of the nineteenth century, long after all forms of brass dial had faded from popularity in northern England.

The one-piece dial must have been considerably cheaper if only for the saving in brass castings and finishing work which was involved in the brass

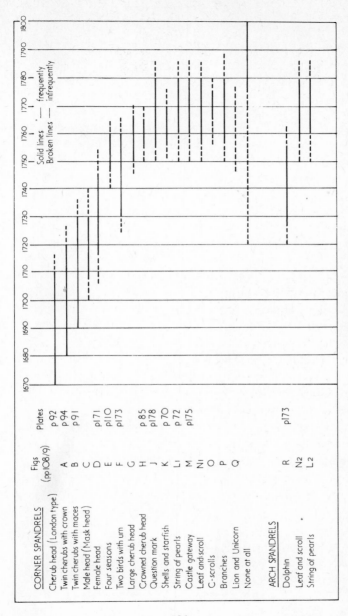

Spandrel dating chart

chapter rings and spandrels of the standard brass dial. The one-piece brass dial probably evolved as a determined effort by the engraving trade to retain the large volume of work it had always enjoyed from the clockmaking trade. The coming of the painted dial posed a very serious threat to the engraving industry. The early painted dial was certainly more legible than the contemporary brass dial, was available in far greater variety of colours and patterns, and was probably cheaper than its brass equivalent. This understandable attempt on the part of the engravers failed ultimately in the south and very rapidly in the north, where after 1780 the brass dial was already in a minority. After 1790 very few brass dial clocks were being made except for the more ostentatious and costly type of mahogany-cased clocks with 'Chippendale' fretting as have survived in Lancashire.

Spandrels form a most helpful guide in assessing the period of a clock, if considered alongside some of the other features already mentioned. We presuppose that the spandrel types which follow are original to their clocks, though of course they can sometimes be replacements. Early styles seem to follow on from London patterns but by mid-century, when the London makers had to a large degree lost interest in the longcase form, various new provincial types flourished.

The earliest provincial form was the cherub's head as in the plate on p 92, based on a London type. This was in use in the late seventeenth century, about 1690–1710. The earliest type commonly met with is the 'twin cherub' one, sometimes called the 'boys and crown' pattern, see spandrels illustration, fig A, and this was used from about 1690 to 1725, perhaps a little later. A second version of the twin cherubs was occasionally used, perhaps more commonly in the south than in the north. This is seen in spandrels illustration, fig B, and differs in so far as the boys here are holding crossed maces below a much larger crown than in the previous example. This crossed maces version was used from about 1690–1730. The twin cherub types would, because of their period, be found almost exclusively on square dials.

All the dates quoted for spandrel periods are intended as a guide and one has to allow a little leeway. However, they do apply fairly closely and a clock purporting to be of the 1780s with twin cherub spandrels just ain't right! Twin cherub spandrels are the most common form of *reproduction* spandrel to be met with. It may be comforting for anyone with a clock lacking one of its four original spandrels to know that it is possible today to buy modern replacements of almost any stock pattern, and the brassfounders are to be congratulated on the faithfulness with which they have copied original patterns and the trouble they have taken for what must be quite a small commercial market.

Next in sequence after the twin cherubs come the adult head or mask patterns, which exist in three or four versions. Used from about 1710 to 1740 they feature a head of a man or woman as a central motif around which is various scrollwork. The reader will forgive me, I hope, if I invent my own name for some of these patterns, as there is no stock name for them and it does simplify reference (see spandrels illustration, figs c and d). The old man tends to appear in the earlier part of the 1710–40 period, and the lady in the later part—age before beauty!

The four seasons pattern was used by some clockmakers in mid-century, about 1745–60, particularly in the north (see spandrels illustration, fig e). The four figures each represent a different season: on p 110 we see spring (top left), summer (top right), autumn (bottom right) and winter (bottom left). There were at least two different patterns for these four seasons spandrels, the figures representing the same general themes but varying a little, especially in size.

A spandrel with two birds (eagles?) supporting an urn was used in the 1730–60 period (see p 173). Again at least two versions exist, superficially similar. In mid-century, about 1750–65, the large cherub head pattern was popular, again mostly with northern makers (see spandrels illustration, fig g). This was a large spandrel often used for larger arched dials with moonwork in the arch, where a bigger-than-average corner space was to be filled. It was frequently partnered with the Dutch minute band. Again more than one version exists. The child's head is large and deeply cast and cannot be confused with the adult head type or the much earlier cherub head of the 1690s. A slightly different type of large cherub-head spandrel is shown in the plate on p 85. This crowned cherub head is smaller and shallower than that in spandrels, fig g and appears mostly on clocks with smaller (10in or 11in) square dials of mid-century, say 1755–65. Sam Roberts used this type.

Another large spandrel much favoured by northern makers, especially on

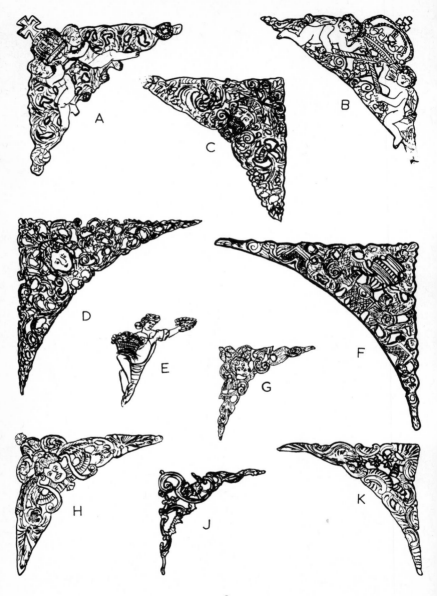

L₁

L₂

M

N₁

N₂

O

P

Q

R

S

Some types of spandrels

Eight-day clock by John
Seddon, Frodsham, c1755

arched dial clocks with arch moonwork in the 1755–80 period, is the question-mark pattern, as in the plate on p 178. A smaller spandrel, mostly used on square dial clocks of about 11in, is that in the plate on p 70, which I call the shells and starfish pattern. It was used between about 1755 and 1770.

By about 1760–5 half a dozen new designs appear which consist largely of floral sprays and branches. That in the plates on p 72 I call the string-of-pearls, as a distinct string of beads runs in one direction from the central area near the rose. This occurs in the 1760–80 period and is almost a certain indi-

110

cation of a 'late' clock. It was mostly on smaller square dials (11 in). Fig M in the spandrels illustration shows another spandrel of the same period and same general style, this one with the pillars of a 'castle gateway' at the centre. Another, in fig N, we call simply the leaf and scroll pattern, same period, same general type.

A few spandrels are rare and one can only assume that they just did not catch the popular imagination. Spandrel, fig S, shows one from a year-clock by John Taylor of Ormskirk of about 1750. Fig Q shows a lion and unicorn pattern (about 1765) which I have only met with twice on simple country clocks. The plate on p 102 shows another unusual one about 1760 of Scottish origin.

Clocks with arched dials often had smaller spandrels set at each side of the arch. In some cases the arch spandrels would be smaller matching versions of the corner ones, though in elongated curved triangular shape. Fig N2 shows a matching arch spandrel used in conjunction with the leaf and scroll corner type. Not all corner spandrels had an arched matching partner and the dolphin pattern (spandrels, fig R, plate on p 173) was sometimes used to partner a variety of such corner ones, mostly pre-1760.

After being cast, spandrels were filed clean to remove any remaining 'rag', and then were polished up and sometimes even gilded, the latter process usually only on more costly clocks. By mid-century the saving of time and cost was becoming increasingly important and many country makers were content to use spandrels without bothering to clear the rag, especially on their cheaper 30-hour clocks. After 1760 well-finished spandrels were usually a sign of a high-quality clock and gilded spandrels even more so.

A form of dial decoration, already mentioned, which appealed to many country clockmakers was the incorporation of a legend or motto. This was frequently of a semi-religious nature and usually reflected on man's need to behave himself in this world, since he might be called to receive his desserts in the next one sooner than expected. Mottoes were usually on brass dial clocks (probably because the clockmaker had closer control over the engraving than he had when ordering a painted dial from further afield) and most appear in the 1760–90 period. Rhymes and mottoes seem to have been more common in the north than the south. One used by Thomas Read of Tarporley about 1770 runs:

Lo, here I stand, all in thy sight
To tell the hours of day and night
Do thou a warning take by me
And serve thy God as I serve thee.

Several north country makers used variations on this verse. *Time flies, pursue it man, for why, thy days are but a span* was a legend used by several Lancashire makers, as was *Time shews the way of life's decay.*

They range from gloomy forebodings to less ponderous phrases such as *Time stayeth not* or, for those who wanted to show off a bit, *Tempus Edax Rerum* (Time the Devourer of All Things), or *Tempus fugit* even.

Another decoration of a more serious nature was a moon dial, which often filled the arch of a clock. This would show the shape of the moon in the sky together with the lunar date. Some clocks from coastal areas incorporated a tidal dial too, simply having an extra band of hour numerals indicating high-tide time engraved on the moon dial and a second indicator arm. Once set, the tidal pointer should remain in sequence, as the tides would run consistently with the moon's phases.

The moon dial on an arched dial clock was, in the earlier period, a brass engraved disc showing through a circle in the arch (see below), later a painted moon disc rotating behind the two characteristic 'camel humps' (see p 113).

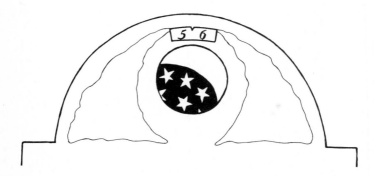

Early type of moon dial. A silvered brass disc passes behind a circular hole in the arch; in this case, a crescent moon is shown half-way through the fifth lunar day

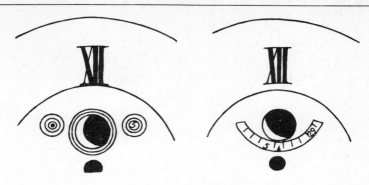

A Halifax or halfpenny moon appeared in two forms; on the left, the moon is seen through a circle in the middle, while the lunar day is shown through a smaller hole on the side. (The hole opposite is simply a dummy for balance.) On the right, the lunar date is seen through an extended segment

Painted arch moon used on both brass and painted dial clocks. Here it shows the twenty-first lunar day

The painted moon disc often incorporated a landscape and seascape alternately between the waxing and waning moon faces. As the old moon waned off to the right, the new moon rose from the left to replace it. On square dials another type of moon was devised to register below the XII hour numeral. This was called a halfpenny moon or a Halifax moon, though it was widely popular all over the north not just around Halifax, and was a clever way of incorporating a moon feature into a square dial. It was also useful in this position, as on 30-hour clocks there was a vacant space

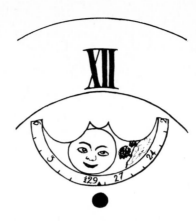

A form of moon half-way between the Halifax type and the arch type. It
was normally used when a decorative moon dial was wanted on a square
dial clock. The moon disc can be painted or silvered brass

there (there being usually no seconds dial on a 30-hour clock). A Halifax
moon was more simply operated than the arched moon, simply knocked on
one notch every twelve hours by a pin on the hour hand pipe. The plate on
p 175 shows a Halifax moon. Occasionally a revolving ball or globular moon
is found in the arch of a clock, but this is very uncommon and required far
more complicated gearing.

The clockmaker's 'signature' on the dial was in a sense a part of the decoration. On very early clocks (late seventeenth century) this might appear
below the chapter ring, and at this period might well be Latinised. Normally it appeared at each side of the VI hour numeral, though it is occasionally found on a plaque attached to the dial centre, or with arched dial
clocks on a boss in the arch. Of course it was not a true signature, nor a fac-
simile of a man's own handwriting, and therefore a dozen different clocks by
the same maker could bear a dozen different representations of his name and
yet each one be quite genuine.

Some country makers, especially north country ones, had the habit of
omitting their place of work and signing their clocks only with their names,
in typical northern disregard of the law, which required the place to be
stated. It is worth noting that this usually applied to clockmakers from the

smaller villages and the reason was perhaps partly because no one would have heard of the place and perhaps too because such a clockmaker might well take his clocks to other local market towns to sell, and so did not wish to pin himself down to one place. We have already noticed this habit with Will Snow of Padside, Yorkshire. Others that come to mind are: David Collier of Etchels, Cheshire; Anthony Batty of Worsborough, Yorks; Jonas Barber the elder of Winster, Westmorland; Thomas Lister the elder of Luddenden, Yorkshire; Francis Moore of Ferrybridge, Yorkshire; John Stancliffe of Barkisland, Yorkshire; and there were very many others.

About 1770 the new white dial was introduced. This was an iron sheet with a surface layer of 'japan' work, that is, a kind of heat-treated paint surface, not true enamel, though sometimes mistakenly referred to as such. The earliest ones we can date with certainty were advertised for the first time in 1772 in the *Birmingham Gazette:*

> Osborne and Wilson, manufacturers of White Clock Dials in Imitation of enamel, in a Manner entirely new, have opened a Warehouse at No 3, in Colmore-Row, Birmingham, where they have an Assortment of the above-mentioned Goods . . .

Birmingham was the place of manufacture of most painted dials, and several specialist dialmaking concerns were soon established there to cater for the phenomenal demand which rapidly developed for this new, more legible and more colourful dial. The clockmaker could not make his own painted dials, but bought them ready-lettered with his name from the specialist dialmakers. Ultimately there were dialmaking specialists in several provincial cities, but Birmingham seems always to have retained the vast bulk of the market.

So great was the demand that after a short time orders were coming into Birmingham from clockmakers in America for shipments of dials. In Britain, too, the demand for white dials grew so quickly that within fifteen years brass dials were almost a thing of the past, although in the south the one-piece silvered brass dial held out even beyond the end of the century.

The new painted dials were probably cheaper than the brass equivalent, but cheapness was not the only, nor even the major, factor. There were many clocks made towards the end of the century where low cost was not of prime importance—musical clocks for instance—yet where painted dials were used. These new dials were undoubtedly popular for their own sakes and not only because of their lower cost.

An 11in square brass dial cost about 12s (Sam Roberts's notebook); an equivalent painted dial cost 8s (in 1800). Other examples of painted dial prices from that date are found in the stock transfer record of Jonas Barber the younger of Winster, Westmorland, who retired in 1800. An arched dial with moonwork in the arch cost £1 2s; an arched dial with landscape painting in the arch cost 16s; a square dial cost 12s—all these in 13in width sizes. By the 1830s, when the average dial width had reached 14in, dials were available in two qualities, the cheaper ones costing about half the price of the better ones. By this time dials were mostly of the arched type, and they ranged between about 15s or 16s to as little as 7s 6d according to quality.

White dials developed in style over the years just as clearly as brass dials had done, and in two major areas—in the style and type of coloured decoration used, and in the numbering system used. Early painted dials were small in width, 11–13in wide; later ones were as much as 15in wide by about 1840. Early ones were largely white with a little coloured decoration in the corners and arch; such themes as a bird, spray of flowers, roses or strawberries all appear commonly from about 1770 to 1800. By 1800 the coloured decoration was a little bolder and had spread out to cover a little more of the white background. In the 1800–20 period there was a great fondness for patterns in the corners, or seashells and seaweed, and in the arch there was often a vignette scene, that is a circular or oval panel containing a painting of, for example, Justice with her scales, Brittania, or some other 'painted lady'. By about 1830 the colour had spread further so that the arch was often filled with a complete painting, a landscape, or a scene from the bible, and the corners now showed ivy-clad ruins and churches or other pastoral scenes. The white background by this time was almost obliterated by coloured over-painting.

In the 1770–1800 period numbering was exactly like the later brass dial type, Roman hours and Arabic minutes marked by dots. In the 1800–20 period the Arabic 5 and 10 minute markers began to be omitted, leaving just 15, 30, 45 and 60 as minute numbers, shown along a full double-circle

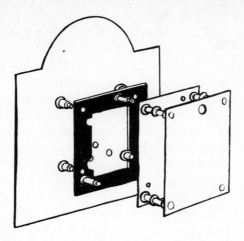

Falseplate fitting showing its position between painted dial and movement

minute band. For a brief spell about 1820 Arabic numbers were used for marking the hours. By 1830 came a return to Roman figures for hour numerals, but by now the minutes ceased to be lettered at all, and this lettering style persisted to the end of British longcase clockmaking—about 1870 in the north, about 1840 in the south. By now it was common knowledge that III past I meant fifteen minutes past one; in the earlier period this was not so and therefore dials were lettered to indicate fifteen minutes past.

With a little practice one can recognise the period of a painted dial clock by its dial, just as one can with a brass dial one. This regular stylistic sequence arose from the centralised nature of the dialmaking industry based in Birmingham, and dialmakers in other towns seem to have copied the style currently fashionable in Birmingham. The dialmakers frequently left their names or initials on their dials and this is often useful as additional evidence with which to confirm a dating by style. Some dials for instance have the initials *W & H* impressed into the back of the arch—the mark of Walker and Hughes who were dialmakers in Birmingham from 1815–35.

Eight-day dials were often, though not always, supplied with an iron 'falseplate' attached—the illustration above shows one—which at the time was called a back-plate! Its purpose was to assist the clockmaker when attaching his movement to the dial in order to avoid the awkwardness of parts of the movement obstructing the fixing positions required by the dial 'feet'. It was mistakenly thought in the past that the falseplate was sold with the movement, and as falseplates often bear the imprint of their makers the mistaken conclusion was drawn that painted dial clocks had 'factory-made' movements. It can readily be observed by anyone taking the trouble to examine the movements behind painted dials of the early period, that they continued in an unbroken tradition in exactly the same form as those by the same makers behind brass dials. For example the Mark Two Will Snow movement (see p 76) appears behind his painted dial clocks (or those of his son), as well as his brass dial ones, and no factory ever made a movement as distinctive as the Snow skeleton-plate type.

Those who are unconvinced will find by referring to a work such as Samuel Harlow's *Clockmakers' Guide* (1813), that he mentions 'the back Plate, generally put on by the Birmingham dial makers' and later goes on to extol the virtues of 'the back plate, commonly used by the Birmingham Dial Makers, which if put on correct, might save the workman a great deal of trouble'. He even illustrates one.

By the 1820s, of course, mass production with its resultant lowering of costs had begun to influence clockmaking to a considerable degree. This meant that increasingly it became an economic proposition for the clock-maker to buy-in more and more of his parts ready made. Hence, later clocks do contain a higher proportion of standardised 'factory-made' parts. On clocks after about 1820 it is increasingly correct to attribute many stan-dardised clock parts to a factory origin, often a Birmingham origin, and by now many movements and dials were being supplied more or less complete with just the finishing and assembly work to be done by the 'clockmaker'. Later clocks therefore seldom needed a falseplate bracket.

One must admit that there is not the same mechanical interest to be found in longcase clocks made after 1830 because of this standardisation, although of course the interest for very many clock-lovers is not a mechanical one. Naturally owners of these later clocks are fond of them, especially if they are family heirlooms, but the clock-collector finds it a little difficult to enthuse about them. There is more real interest, in my opinion, in the indi-viduality of a 30-hour cottage clock by Sam Roberts or Will Snow than in the most ostentatious 8-day clock of 1840, where the name on the dial has scarcely any meaning as far as the making of the clock was concerned.

The hands of a clock are another helpful guide to period, though one where experience is needed, as hands can so often be incorrect replacements of broken originals. Fifty years ago a restorer seeking to replace a broken hand seems often to have dipped into his box of spares, pulled out the first thing he saw of the required length and fastened it on, regardless of what type of clock it had originally belonged to. This means that today probably the most frequent fault to be found on clocks is an incorrect hand or hands.

Early hands were made of steel, and brass dial clocks always had steel hands. Extremely rare exceptions to this rule do exist—Thomas Lister the elder of Halifax, for instance, preferred brass hands, although shaped in contemporary patterns normally associated with steel. On clocks which had a centre-seconds hand or a centre-date hand these were often in brass to help distinguish them from the normal (steel) hour and minute ones. Brass hands on a brass dial clock can generally be considered to be incorrect replacements.

Early steel hands did not 'match' in the modern way; that is, the hour and minute hands were quite dissimilar, probably as an aid to distinguishing more easily one from the other. The development of stylistic features such as hands and dials was not a chance happening, but all the time one can see the underlying reason for it, usually arising from the position held by the household clock amongst society at large combined with the ever-increasing importance of cutting corners to keep cost, and therefore retail price, down to the lowest possible level.

The hour hand began life in roughly an ace-of-spades shape, symmetrical, finely pierced and fretted, filed clean, chamfered, bevelled—a superb piece of craftsmanship involving many hours of work. The one hand of a single-handed clock was just like a contemporary hour hand but had a shaped tail to help with leverage when resetting the time (see plate on p 91). The earlier and finer the clock, the better would be the quality of the hands. An 8-day clock of say 1700 would have a superb hour hand, as can be seen in the examples shown in the plates on p 92 and p 94, provincial work would generally be less elaborate than London work, largely because of the cost factor. A single-hander of the same time (30-hour of course) would have a

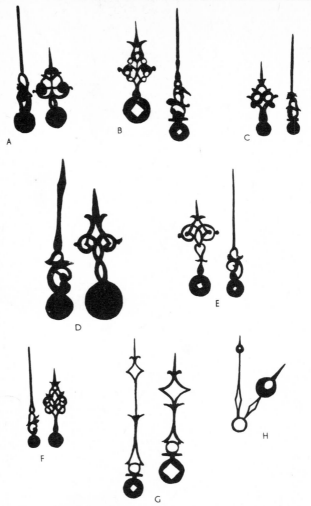

An assortment of steel hands showing patterns found on country clocks of known date

A 1745-50   E 1770
B 1746   F 1772
C 1750-60   G 1800
D 1767   H 1847

simpler hand with less elaborate piercing, both for reasons of cost and also because it would need to be sturdier to stand up to the rougher treatment it would receive in use.

The early minute hand would be asymmetrical, pierced from its base for perhaps a third of its length and terminating in a straight pointer. Hands were normally called pointers at the time. The illustrations show some typical examples taken from a variety of makers. Each man had his own ideas of design, but all tended to follow the conventional pattern and hence hands are very helpful guides to period.

By about 1770 the minute hand's straight pointer section has developed into a serpentine shape (see p 102). The hour hand by now has become a slighter thing, perhaps less elaborately pierced, and the design has generally thinned down a little. The year 1800, give or take five years, marks the introduction of matching hands, still made of steel of course. Examples are shown in the hands illustration, fig G and H. Some were still cut by hand by the clockmaker, but they were now increasingly stamped out by machine. Matching steel hands cost 7d a pair in 1802.

By 1825 brass hands had arrived in matching pattern, initially resembling matching steel ones in design, but later developing into more intricate styles, as the illustrations show. From now on steel hands were quite exceptional (except perhaps on regulators) and matching brass hands were used right to the end of longcase clockmaking. I cannot recall ever having seen matching brass hands on clocks earlier than about 1820, where I was satisfied that they were original. In 1822 Isaac Simpson of Chorley, Lancashire, received an order for a clock which specifically requested 'steel fingers'— the implication being that by this time a choice of steel or brass was available. Brass hands cost 8d a pair in 1835, seconds hands $2\frac{1}{2}$d each.

One often reads how well-balanced hands would 'fit' the clock dial exactly so that the hour hand just reached as far as the inner edge of the chapter ring and the minute hand just reached as far as the minute band. This seems a commonsense idea and was apparently traditional London practice. However, large numbers of provincial clocks have hands which do not observe these rules (I am speaking of hands apparently original to the clock), and this leads one to believe that country clockmakers were not nearly so particular about this as their London cousins might have been.

Bracket clock by Barnaby Dammant, Colchester, c1725

So far we have discussed almost exclusively the longcase clock, which was *the* British clock. Table clocks *were* made in the provinces. They are usually called bracket clocks, and whilst some undoubtedly stood on small wall brackets, the fact that many have their engraved backplates visible through the glass-panelled back of the case shows that they were intended for use on a table, chest of drawers or cabinet top. Apart from the point-lessness of engraving a surface which would be hidden against the wall, the fact that most bracket clocks have the old verge escapement is evidence that they were meant to be moved about, not fixed on a permanent 'bracket' shelf.

Provincial bracket clocks of the eighteenth century or earlier are scarce. Those of us who have made a hobby of research into the clockmakers of in-dividual areas have recorded only a very few in each county—for example, Yorkshire had half a dozen, Cumberland two, Westmorland none, Lanca-shire had half a dozen and Suffolk no more than a handful. In the nineteenth century the numbers increased partly because, as we have seen, increasing mechanisation and resultant lowering of costs enabled local clockmakers to buy-in ready-made parts, thereby bringing the costly spring clock down to a price range that customers could afford. Bracket clocks are not very im-portant numerically in the provincial British clock scene until after 1820, although because of their scarcity they are 'important' in the sense of being noteworthy. Styles of dials followed more or less those of the longcase clocks, which we have already examined in detail, and in this book bracket clocks do not merit further treatment.

CHAPTER 6
CASES AND COSTS

It was suggested earlier that cases for longcase clocks probably originated with the need to support the heavy twin driving weights of Ahasuerus Fromanteel's 1658 pendulum clocks of 8-day duration and longer. A floor-standing box container was safer and stronger than a wall-mounted bracket, and additionally kept out the dust. Further it could be made to lock and thereby prevent anyone but the master from meddling with what then was a very costly piece of scientific equipment. (It has always been the prerogative of the master of the house to fiddle with such things.) A rectangular box was all that was needed, high enough to allow the required fall of the weight, wide enough to house the dial and allow the pendulum clearance.

The illustration shows such a box, but we can imagine without too much difficulty why Fromanteel clocks, and the like, are not found in such boxes. The clocks were very costly items; their purchasers were essentially royalty, nobility, and wealthy gentry, who would not tolerate a mere box in their homes however marvellous its contents. The 'packaging' was very import-ant, hence Fromanteel and his contemporaries had to provide a box which was beautiful as well as functional. The typical Fromanteel case illustrated is slim, neat, small, about 5ft 6in or a little higher, in black ebony or ebonised pearwood, adorned with gilded or even solid silver mounts—a jewel box to contain a jewel!

Within ten years the coming of the anchor escapement and long pendu-lum necessitated a wider trunk to give clearance to the pendulum bob. To retain overall balance this meant increasing the height to 7ft or more. New and more extravagant tastes followed on from the Fromanteel prototypes,

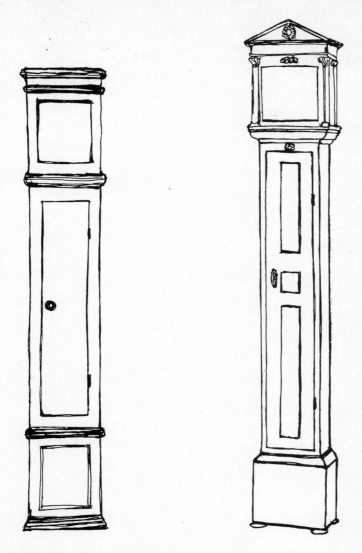

(Left) A coffin case, simply a protective box; *(right)* type of case favoured by the Fromanteels

which we must remember were conceived in a more restrained Puritan atmosphere. Marquetry cases, sometimes described unkindly as being like wallpapering with wood, introduced a much more spectacular and ostentatious period lasting for perhaps forty years from about 1675. This was essentially only in London and the finest provincial work.

So, where does the 'coffin' case fit in? The answer is that a good many of the earlier provincial clocks of the late seventeenth century began life in primitive straight-up-and-down box cases of this sort, because the preceding remarks applied only to casework in London and the finest and costliest provincial clocks. Clocks do still survive in these crude coffin cases—I have already mentioned the one by Edward East. I have seen a couple of others and very much regret not having bought one such when I had the opportunity some years ago. Many must have been scrapped when increasing sophistication of taste called for something with more style to it. These box cases are about as primitive as a plank kist and exceedingly rare today, yet probably more important in the historical development of country cases than the more ornate marquetry cases made for palaces, which by comparison survive in very large numbers. There is so little 'style' to such a coffin case that turning it upside down would hardly alter the shape.

Of course the marquetry case is immeasurably 'better' and far more desirable to the great majority of people today. Most collectors would not want a coffin case as a gift. The old saying is quite true: that a seventeenth-century rabbit-hutch is still only a rabbit-hutch! But of course seventeenth-century clockowners were not considering the whims of twentieth-century clock-collectors when they scraped up enough for a coffin case and in a realistic history of clocks, a coffin case would be a prize item.

The later years of the seventeenth century saw the appearance of toned-down versions of the contemporary London case *outline*, same shape but smaller, simpler and of cheaper woods—oak principally, sometimes pine, as in the plate above. Provincial cases from 1690 to 1740 or later might well look like this with or without the canopy or dome above the hood according to the whim of the maker. Sometimes such cases were in walnut, sometimes walnut veneer, sometimes London-style marquetry or highly decorative veneers of laburnum or olivewood. Mostly, however, cost and setting dictated that they would be of plain oak, which is virtually immune

(Left) Oak case of Shepley clock, c1710; *(right)* plain-oak case of Wolley clock, c1745

to woodworm. (English oak only gets worm in sapwood streaks or in denatured parts such as rotting feet.) Some cottage clocks were still housed in cases of this simple pattern until the nineteenth century, although they became a little less slender as the years went by, and the lenticle glass in the door (by means of which one could see at a glance if the clock were going) had more or less disappeared by 1740.

As I mentioned earlier, 1720 saw the beginnings of the arched dial, and really it was this arch addition which began the complexities of case design. The square dial clock case could have run on for 150 years almost unchanged in outline, but the arch was a sign of innovation, demonstrating the desire to be different; it was new, it was daring, and it immediately gathered a huge following of those who wanted to be in the forefront of fashion. From now on it was a competition—how to be different on the one hand, how to be like so-and-so on the other.

It is difficult to know where to begin with provincial arched dial casework, but perhaps the basic shape is a good starting-point. The arch was semi-circular and the line was echoed in the case hood-top outline, as in the plate on p 96. This one I call the southern traditional domed top (you see the double-dome on Queen Anne bureaux) and I suppose it began about 1720

Hood styles. On the left, a pagoda top, sometimes called a bell top or tea-caddy top; on the right, the architectural top

and persisted with a little variety until the end of the century. The domed top was the obvious shape determined from the dial. However, just as the square dial clock had sometimes had a decorative cresting or pagoda top or tea-caddy top just for variety, so too the domed top soon acquired its top hat addition, often as an 'optional extra' in the design. This is shown in the first of the two hoods illustrated which is nothing more than a domed hood with a bell top (so called, since those with a well-developed imagination can see in it the outline of a bell). The bell top, sometimes called a tea-caddy top, started about 1725–30 and ran right through to perhaps 1810, often accompanied by an arch-topped trunk door.

Thirty-hour clock by James Thompson, Darlington, c1785

Examples of changing door shapes. The general period date is followed in each case by the actual date of the example:

A 1690–1820 (1740)   F 1760–70 (1775—Lancs)   K 1800–25 (1820)
B 1725–1825 (1775)   G 1760–90 (1770—Bristol) L 1830–50 (1840)
C 1730–80 (1745)   H 1760–90 (1770—Bristol) M 1820–45 (1830)
D 1750–1810 (1765)   I 1765–95 (1780)   N 1830–50 (1840)
E 1750–1800 (1770)   J 1785–1830 (1820)   O 1830–50 (1850)

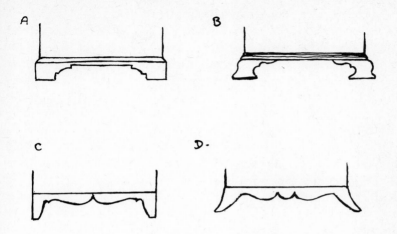

Styles of clock case feet: A Simple bracket feet; B Ogee bracket feet;
C Semi-French feet; D French feet

The second hood displays a later architectural top sometimes met with in
the second half of the eighteenth century, though never a common style.
Another version of it is the break-arch top (see Page 129) which is really
only a variation of the dome top, broken at the centre with a finial support.
This is found in the 1760–1820 period. Perhaps the commonest of all the
later hood tops, especially in the north, is the swan-necked pediment, as in
the plate on p 134. This can occur on square dial clocks but is more common
on arched dial ones. It began about the middle of the eighteenth century and
lasted right through until 1870. A plain flat top can occur on an arched dial
hood, but this is uncommon and not often very graceful. It can also be an indication that a tall clock has been shortened by removing its swan-necks or
other pediment and replacing them with an all-round plain moulding.

The hood shapes just examined are where most variety is found. The door
shape can also help to indicate the period. Early doors are flat-topped, long,
slim, fill the whole of the trunk space, often have a half-round beading
round the edge and a lenticle glass (see plates on p 125, 127 and 130).
Gradually the door top takes on experimental shapes, a simple arch, a wavy

top, or a multi-pointed 'gothic' top. The diagrams give an indication of the periods, which of course overlap greatly.

Clocks stand either on a plinth, a plinth cut into a simple form of bracket foot, or sometimes shaped ogee feet. Splayed 'French' feet began about 1770, although they are more common in the nineteenth century. Bun feet very occasionally occurred on late seventeenth-century examples but big 'chunky' bun feet were a late Victorian feature.

An unusual form of longcase clock, which one tends to associate mostly with Wales, though they were made elsewhere, was a dresser clock. The centre part of the dresser rack was built to take a clock which was inserted into the woodwork so that the pendulum and weight(s) fitted into a channel down the back. Sometimes the clock-housing cupboard part was an ordinary longcase trunk and hood built into the dresser rack. An example of a dresser clock is in the Welsh Folk Museum at St Fagans, Cardiff, made by Moses Evans of Llangerniew in 1797. It is not unknown for antique dealers to insert a baseless clock case into a dresser rack and, hey-presto, a rare dresser clock!

So far we have discussed shapes and outlines, let us consider the woods used. Before 1740–50 cases were mainly oak, less frequently pine, which was cheaper but far less durable being prone to woodworm. Pine was always sold painted or stained or grained, usually being made to look like a more costly wood such as mahogany. Pine cases were painted with simple household paint—kitchen green, or teapot brown if you like—occasionally with over-painted decoration such as flowers. Such cases must not be confused with lacquered or japanned cases, which underwent a far more sophisticated treatment, were made for altogether grander surroundings, and were japanned on an *oak* carcase, not softwood. White pine, waxed or stripped pine and deal are all terms used to describe the same thing, that is a softwood case, which has had all its paint scraped off and stands now as naked as the day it left the joiner's shop with all its knots, nail-heads and filler showing. Stripped pine is fashionable today, but we should realise that it was never intended to be sold as bare wood and that in stripping it we are totally changing its character to satisfy 'trendy' tastes. One might as well deal in stripped oak, stripped walnut or stripped mahogany.

Pine cases were made from the earliest times to about 1830, gradually dying out as tastes became more sophisticated. A pine clock was often bought for the kitchen or servants' quarters or for a cottage. I read somewhere that pine cases mostly date from after the 1760s. This is true, though misleading. The reason that very few early pine cases survive is not because they were not made then, but because hungry country woodworms have eaten them. Those pine cases which survive today mostly survive only by virtue of their once having had a painted surface, which helped to keep out worm. A simple pine case might have cost 10–15s in the eighteenth century.

An oak case was more costly at about £1.00, again for a very simple type as in the plate on p 127. More elaborations naturally would make it more costly. Later oak cases (after about 1760) usually have some mahogany trimming and banding just for variety.

Walnut cases appeared from the late seventeenth century, mostly in the form of veneer. Walnut cases are rather strange so far as their distribution is concerned. Most English walnut was used up by about 1730, although in the south of England cases of solid plain-grain walnut are found even in the later eighteenth century. In the north at this time, walnut is very uncommon, the reason probably being the easy availability of mahogany shipped into northern ports such as Liverpool. The southern English casemakers must have obtained their walnut from European ports. Walnut, of course, was much softer than oak and far more prone to worm. Hence, many walnut cases have perished over the years. Mahogany was available in this country even in the late seventeenth century, but was very scarce and costly. By 1730, however, it was more abundant and cheaper and was rapidly becoming popular. It came from the West Indies and was brought in through ports such as Liverpool, which may account for its being more common in, for example, Lancashire than Suffolk. By the 1730s Gillows, the Lancaster cabinet makers, were already exporting mahogany clock cases back to the West Indies out of Liverpool.

Mahogany cases are not often found before 1750, but by 1765–70 they were quite common on better clocks, both in the solid and in veneers. The finest cases had choice veneers set onto a solid mahogany carcase. Later, especially in the nineteenth century, they were veneered onto pine. Mahogany was the most costly wood for cases and oak remained the standard wood for simpler and cheaper design, such as the 30-hour cottage clock.

Mahogany case of Lawrie clock,
c1760

Lacquer cases, or japanned cases as they are sometimes called, were perhaps more popular in London and the south than in the north. The background colour was most commonly black, sometimes green, blue or red,
and very occasionally yellow. Onto this background was applied raised
decorative goldwork often in oriental style. The wood base was oak. Such
cases were no doubt very costly when new and would, perhaps, have been
preferred for a country gentleman's mansion, in an altogether more spectacular setting than the average provincial clock. One normally associates
them with the period 1740–65 and most often with arched dial 8-day clocks
with brass dials, of course, at this period. It would certainly seem incongruous to house a square dial 30-hour cottage clock in such a costly and
more pompous type of case. Whilst the finish of a wooden case improves
with age (and care), that of a lacquer one deteriorates, which means that
most lacquer cases one sees today are in a very shabby state.

I once bought a clock of about 1760 by Nathaniel Brown of Manchester
in a carved black oak case. Carved cases have been much maligned and mis-
understood in the past, but despite widespread rumours that such cases were
mostly carved by Victorian devotees of the chisel, I was satisfied that this
case was original in construction and carving, just as I believe that many of
its contemporaries were. The vendor told me some of its history.

At some time in its past the clock had accompanied its owner on a journey
to the Far East, where he was a planter, and it had survived the ruinous cli-
mate there until he returned to England on retiring. At this time he had
meticulously dismantled the clock, wrapped every part in sacking and carefully packed them. I was rather alarmed to see that he had done exactly the
same with the case, having knocked it down to single-piece components,
numbered each piece, wrapped them all in sacking and packed them into tea
chests. The owner had subsequently died and the clock had remained in that
state in storage for many years until I bravely rumaged through the sacks,
moths and spiders and agreed to buy a 200-year-old do-it-yourself-by-
numbers clock kit! The original glass was still intact in the hood door!

I had several weeks of amusement and frustration in trying to reassemble
the clock and miraculously it was complete apart from one or two bits of
broken beading. However, it taught me something about clock case construction. The bracket feet could be seen to be replacements in a mahogany-

135

like wood, presumably made on arrival in the Indies. The case backboard was also an ingenious replacement, presumably made after the case had reached the Far East. It was obviously designed to avoid troubles when dismantling the clock for the return journey to England; it was made in small sections, each being held in place by wooden turnbuckles and being therefore very easy to dismantle.

It seemed to me that the carving must have been original. It is difficult to explain just why I got this impression but one example occurs to me. Around the lip of the top trunk moulding, at the point where the hood slides on, was a thin band of carved gadroon-type moulding for decoration. The hood slid on over the top of this moulding, leaving the carved portion showing, which matched the rest of the case decoration. If this carved moulding had *not* been present (of course uncarved cases do not have such a moulding at all) the hood sliding tracks would have been too big and the hood would have sat very sloppily and insecurely. In other words the hood must have been made to fit *with* this carved moulding in place.

I have seen many other carved cases which I felt sure were original in construction and carving, mostly on brass dial clocks of the 1760–90 period. When I think of perhaps twenty clocks that I know by Thomas Lister the younger of Halifax, in the region of half of them are in carved cases, which is far too high a proportion to be pure chance 'Victorian' carving. Ask any clock enthusiast in the Halifax area and he could tell of such clocks by the Stancliffes, Battys, John Pattison, William Lister and others of this area and period.

The plate shows a very fine example of a carved, black oak case with its apparently original clock by John Stancliffe of Barkisland (Halifax) made about 1765. Some further details of this are given later on, but consider for a moment the cost of such a case. Take any 2in square section, imagine the time involved in drawing out and measuring the design in that section and imagine the time taken to carve that section. Then consider that there are almost 1,000 such sections in the whole case! This must have been far more costly than lacquer work and of course far more durable. Perhaps they were a northern alternative to lacquer, which seems to have been more popular in the south.

Carved oak is 'in' at present. Ten years ago nobody in the trade wanted it,

136

(Left) Carved oak case with clock by John Stancliffe, Halifax, c1765; *(right)* oak case of Lister clock, c1760

although of course that did not affect the high regard which country clock owners had always had for their clocks. Today carved cases are in great demand and this demand must surely increase as it is gradually recognised that the stereotyped attitudes of fifty years ago, which dismissed them all as 'Victorian', just do not hold up to examination.

While a country clockmaker was seldom concerned with cases, a town or city clockmaker would normally have a sales shop and would be expected to supply a clock complete with case. Examples of priced records that we can find confirm the two systems. Let us consider one or two examples.

We know that a mid-eighteenth-century 30-hour clock ran between about £2 3s and £2 10s *without* a case. One exists by William Roberts of Otley, Yorkshire, with the original receipt pasted inside the case door: 'This clock was settled the 7th Oct 1758 prise £2 3 6d'. The term 'settled' suggests that some bargaining was involved. Such a clock would normally be housed in a plain oak case, costing about £1 to £1 10s. So that, for a straightforward 30-hour square dial clock in oak we are talking in terms of perhaps £3 10s to £4 in all, backed up by a guarantee for, in some cases, as long as *seven years*! (Michael Quesnel, a clockmaker in Jersey, guaranteed a clock, which he sold in 1771, for *ten* years 'accidents excepted').

The coming of the painted dial may well have lowered the price slightly. In 1791 the Chaplin family of clockmakers of Bury St Edmunds advertised in the *Ipswich Journal:* '30 hour clocks with minutes [ie two hands] and day of the month in wainscot [ie oak] or walnut tree cases at £3 13 6d'. It is interesting to note that walnut was offered as an option in the south as late as this and was no more costly than oak. It is seldom found so late in the north and one might have expected it to be more costly than oak.

Looking at 8-day examples the price range must run far higher according to how elaborate the clock and the case. Sam Roberts charged about £4 for his 8-day clocks, probably quite simple ones, *without* cases of course, and £4 remained about the standard price of a basic 8-day clock. Just as an illustration of a contemporary example and as an indication of the nature of trade rivalry, I will quote the following two advertisements from the weekly *Newcastle Journal* of March 1766:

John Walker, clock and watch maker in the Close, Newcastle

To the public:

Having from repeated experiments during the course of eight years invented a perfect machine for cutting and finishing the movements of a clock with more accuracy and expedition than when performed by the hand, and at the same time the machinery made more simple by a reduction in the number of wheels has now at his shop (for sale) a large quantity of clocks cut by this machine which he finds answer better than the common eight-day clock. Whoever pleases to favour him with their orders may depend on being punctually served in most reasonable manner, by their humble servant John Walker. NB The price of an eight-days clock is £3 13s 6d [without case of course]

The following week appeared:

D. Patterson

This is to acquaint the publicThat as all the wheels of a clock may be freed (or teeth rounded up) by a workman in four or five hours the expense sav'd by the so much boasted finishing engines must be very trifling: and being unwilling curtailing of making slight ordinary skeleton clocks to debase so valuable an art, or my own character, I continue to give experienced journeymen high prices to enable them to make good work. Therefore cannot propose selling eight-day clocks for less than four guineas (£4 4s 0d). Hoping the judicious will not scruple that price for so useful and durable machine which if well made may probably last 100 years. All who are pleased to favour me with their orders may depend upon being served with substantial clocks of excellent workmanship at the above prices by David Patterson clock and watch maker in Sunderland.

The reader will note that John Walker's invention was for 'finishing' the wheels, ie rounding the teeth. Engines for cutting out the wheel teeth had been used for many years. David Patterson's scathing remarks about 'slight skeleton clocks' brings to mind the skeleton plate nature of Will Snow's movements.

The 8-day clock then averaged £4 or £4 4s; with a simple case perhaps

£5 to £5 10s. The advertisement by the Chaplins of Bury St Edmunds in 1791 offered: 'Best new eight-day clocks in square case [ie square dial], either wainscot or walnut-tree at £5.00, the same in arched case at £5 5s 5d. New eight-day clocks in mahogany cases at £6 6s 6d, the same with moon phases at £6 16s 6d.' These would almost certainly be painted dial clocks.

From the basic 8-day in a simple case one could set whatever upper financial limit one was willing to pay according to how spectacular a clock or how grand a case was wanted. Thomas Moore of Ipswich (Suffolk) sold a quarter chiming clock in 1741 'a curious eight-day quarter clock in a fine walnut case' for £16 16s. A 'quarter clock' was probably a quarter-hour chimer, ie a ting-tang clock. The word 'curious' is often used in the eighteenth century in connection with clocks and watches and does not have its present-day meaning of 'odd' but, from the root word 'cura', means made 'with great care' and hence the modern equivalent might be 'fine'. A really good mahogany case could cost as much as £10 *without* a clock.

Competition for business was keen and each man did his best to undercut his rivals in price. Nevertheless there was a strong feeling of comradeship in the trade. The spirit which brought about the founding of the Clockmakers' Company existed just as strongly in the provinces, though less formally, and gave rise to such sentiments as clockmaker Richard France of Warrington (Lancashire) expressed in his 1740 will: 'to the clockmakers that come to my burial, each a pair of gloves'.

Whilst the longcase or grandfather clock was always the main British provincial clock, other types were made, particularly by town makers, and these were mostly offered for the home which wanted a second or even third clock. Bracket clocks became cheaper in the nineteenth century, probably because of mass production. There were also spring-driven wall clocks, plain, simple, non-striking, the equivalent of a modern office clock or kitchen clock. The Chaplins' 1791 advertisement offered 'exceeding neat new spring dials in mahogany cases at £3 13s 6d'. These were probably round dial wall clocks but notice that they are as costly as the 8-day longcase and would not be such good timekeepers and of course were non-strikers.

An average 30-hour grandfather clock and case at £4, an 8-day one with case at £6—these prices seem a little comical today, unless we convert them into their modern monetary value by multiplying by forty. This shows that

Wall clock by Hedge, Colchester, c1770

the costs were then equivalent to what would today be £160 and £240 respectively. How many of us would today be willing to pay that kind of money for an ordinary modern household clock? Very few. This is because clocks have become ever cheaper over the years with increasing mass-production bringing down manufacturing costs. This downward cost trend was already evident by the mid-nineteenth century, when the larger 8-day clocks complete with fancier mahogany-veneered case could be bought for about £5 5s. By mid-century, however, British clockmakers had lost the price battle to cheaper imported clocks from Europe and America. The cheapest American wall clocks sold in this country at 15s. No British clock could compete with that.

A round wall dial clock is shown above. They are often called English dial clocks or simply 'Dial Clocks'. Mostly they had a simple circular case almost all the front of which was taken up by the circular dial. The circular door was often of brass. They are the antique equivalent of what we would today regard as a school, office, kitchen, or railway waiting-room clock. They range from about 11 or 12in in diameter to exceptionally 16in in diameter. They are spring driven, the movement being housed behind the dial so that all one actually sees is the dial. Mostly they were timepieces only (ie non-striking) but occasionally they were built with strikework—of course the non-striker was cheaper to make. Many had the old verge escapement, but some had the anchor escapement and these required more precise wall-fixing to keep them in beat.

These dial clocks were made from about 1780, but most date between about 1810 and 1835. The dials were of silvered brass on the earlier (or better-quality later) ones; later ones usually had painted dials similar to longcase clock dials, though painted in just plain white without any decoration. Hand patterns are similar to those on longcase clocks, though matching steel hands seem to have persisted longer on clocks of this type.

Some dial clocks have a box-like structure below to accept a longer pendulum and these are known as 'Drop Dials'. By the 1840s the manufacture of English dial clocks gave way to mass-produced imported wall clocks from Germany and America.

There were other native wall clocks, which, though far less common, deserve a mention. These were the longcase clocks which were used without cases as wall clocks, carrying on the tradition of the old lantern clock. These were mostly 30-hour clocks, both of birdcage and of plated construction. Occasionally a customer would want to use such a clock as a wall clock for reasons of economy in saving the cost of the case or the space it might need. These are sometimes called hook-and-spike clocks, being hung from a hook on a nail in the wall and having a sharp spike at the back of each side to grip the plaster. Sometimes they are called wag-on-the-wall clocks, though this term seems to mean different things to different people. The weight and pendulum simply hung down as with the lantern clock.

The next step was to enclose the movement to keep out dirt by encasing the hook-and-spike clock with what was really no more than the hood of a long case, fitting onto a wooden wall-bracket. These were called hood clocks. It is a mistake to think that a hood clock was a transitional stage between lantern and true longcase clocks, as hood clocks are almost always later than the earliest longcase ones. The hood was simply a cheaper expedient than buying a full longcase. Weight and pendulum still hung down for the cat to play with. Hood clocks are uncommon, probably because, like all forms with uncovered weights, they were a little impractical and they probably had a high destruction rate. However, one does find that some 30-hour clocks, now living in proper longcases, show signs that they once carried the hook and spikes, thereby betraying their true origins.

The hood clock then is a hybrid form—sometimes a lantern clock wanting to be a longcase; sometimes a longcase clock trying to be a lantern. It was a partial solution and did not last. Hood clocks are usually of the eighteenth century and can be dated by the normal stylistic features of dial, movement, etc. Often they incorporate an alarm, a carry-over again from the lantern clock.

There was another type of wall clock which was used in coaching houses and taverns. Sometimes they are called 'Stage Coach Clocks' or 'Tavern Clocks', sometimes 'Act of Parliament Clocks'. They were large wall clocks, 4–5ft long with a large dial usually without a glass cover. They were weight driven and usually non-striking. Cases were often of mahogany, although some were lacquered. They had long slim trunks, sometimes straight sided, sometimes fiddle shaped, and they swelled out into large circular tops to accommodate the over-sized dials. Occasionally the dial was black with white numbering. Sometimes the top was surrounded by or surmounted by carving. These clocks are not often seen today.

The term 'Act of Parliament' comes from the fact that in 1797 an Act imposed a tax on all clocks and watches of 5s a year. It is popularly supposed that this led to an increase in the manufacture and use of tavern clocks and public clocks generally, as private citizens declined to use domestic clocks. How serious was the effect on the trade output may be seen from the evidence given to a committee of enquiry. William Tarleton of Liverpool testified how prior to the act he employed as many as 300 men and apprentices and how he now (1798) had only half of these and they were working only a three-day week. His output of twenty gold watches per year had stopped completely and his output of twenty silver watches each week was down to half with many even of those remaining unsold. Thomas Johnstone of Prescot, Lancashire had for thirty years made gold watch hands. His sales figures fell from over £800 a quarter to just over £200 a quarter because of the Act. His workforce of forty was cut to twenty and even then 'they had nothing to do when I came away on Friday'.

The clock trade suffered so seriously that the Act was repealed after only a year, but somehow the term 'Act of Parliament Clock' stuck. In fact we know that clocks of this sort were made for a good many years before the Act. 'The Art of Making Clocks and Watches' (the illustration on p 150) dated 1748, provides a good example.

CHAPTER 7

FAKES

In a situation where clocks bearing famous names may fetch several thousand pounds and where restorers have the skills necessary to reproduce accurately all the parts of such clocks, the possibility of a famous name being added to a bogus mechanism seems to me to be very high. The temptations are obvious. Fortunately, in provincial clocks the situation is less hazardous. Here we are talking, at most, in terms of perhaps hundreds of pounds and the rewards, and therefore incentive, to serious forgery are much less. Just as this likelihood of forgery is much lower in provincial than in London clocks, so too it is lower in 30-hour than in 8-day brass dial clocks, and lower still in painted dial clocks than in brass dial ones. Those with the talents for forgery are hardly likely to direct them towards clocks of low value. Notice I said *serious* forgery, by which I mean a studied and deliberate attempt to either make a clock from scratch or convert an existing clock into a more valuable item. However, it may surprise you to learn that I would reckon that perhaps as many as one provincial brass dial clock in eight is a fake! We shall shortly consider the reasons for this, but first let those of us, who have grown weary of being told that provincial clocks are not in the same league as London ones, take heart from the fact that provincial fakes are not in the same league at all as London fakes. Provincial fakes are almost always very 'hammy' jobs, easy to spot, and giving no trouble at all—if you know what to watch out for. In outlining the danger signs it may help if we consider the types of fake and the reasons behind them.

First the outright fake, the clock made today by a modern craftsman in the manner of 200 years ago or more, is almost non-existent amongst provincial clocks, because, as has been explained, there is simply not enough money in them. Anyone making a fake in this way would surely have the knowledge to add in a famous London name. It is worth mentioning that there have always been a few people ready to pass off their clocks as being something better than they are. Some of the lesser contemporaries of certain of the more famous seventeenth-century London makers are said to have sold works falsely bearing these famous names. In 1682 the Clockmakers' Company wardens seized various clocks bearing apparently invented names, 'all which names are greatly suspected to be invented or fobbed'.

One category of fakes that one does encounter in provincial clocks is that of the conversion. The great bulk (perhaps up to 80 per cent of all such clocks) of brass dial provincial clocks were, as we know, of 30-hour duration. Fifty years or more ago such 30-hour clocks, if broken or very worn, were not worth the cost and trouble of repairing. I have heard from a number of men who worked in the trade at that time of the following common practice. Rather than repair worn-out parts, they would consider it easier to fit a totally different movement in good condition. Whilst they were at it they often thought it an advantage to use an 8-day rather than 30-hour movement to make the winding less of a chore. In the local saleroom a big painted dial 8-day clock could be bought for 7s 6d. They bought one just for its movement, left the unwanted case behind, and fitted the mid-nineteenth-century 8-day movement onto the mid-eighteenth-century dial, satisfied with having done a good conversion job cheaply.

I recall examining a clock by one of the numbers men, which happened to be dated on the dial 1763. The 8-day movement was attached by means of an iron falseplate (these were supplied with painted dials only, but were often used by fakers in assisting to fit a wrong movement to a dial). The falseplate was impressed with the words 'Osborne's Manufactory, Birmingham', which did not come into being till 1778. These sort of giveaway signs are often there, if we trouble to look.

Today we may despise or ridicule this sort of conversion operation. However, there is one aspect of these older conversions which we must recognise and this may make them a little less obnoxious to us. That is that they were not done for profit or deception but as a simple expedient to save cost. The result is the same in that the clock was ruined, but our understanding of the motive may help us view their actions with sorrow rather than anger. Our understanding of the reasons behind these conversions will also help us recognise them since because they were not converted as deliberate fakes, no attempt was made at camouflaging the fact that they were conversions. They are therefore easy to spot. In the example just mentioned, for instance, a modern faker with any knowledge would first of all know better than to use a falseplate fitting, as that in itself is a giveaway on a brass dial. Even if he had not this knowledge, however, he would have had enough sense to use a falseplate without a name on it.

Two faults are usually very obvious on such conversions. Firstly, the dial will have been designed for a 30-hour clock with either a matted centre or (perhaps more commonly) an engraved centre, or sometimes for a single-handed clock. One-handers have the distinctive chapter ring marking quarter-hours, not minutes, and as single-handers were always 30-hour clocks, it follows that an 8-day one must be a conversion. Dials with engraved centres (made for two-handed clocks) usually had a pattern or design in the engraving showing perhaps flowers or a scene. The two winding holes, which converters had to drill through the dial·centre (to allow access for key winding) very often interrupt the engraved design, cutting right through or into the engraved pattern. Nobody in his right mind ever planned a clock dial centre in that way (very few, I should say; see the plate on p 102). A clockmaker did not go to the trouble or cost of engraving a beautiful design only to chop right through it by cutting out winding holes. An engraved centre planned for an 8-day clock was designed so that the two winding holes formed a part of that design, as for instance where these holes each form the centre of a flower-head (see p 178). In other words the holes were cut *prior* to engraving; winding holes cut *after* engraving and breaking into the design are an almost certain sign of a switched movement, ie a fake.

With matted dial centres no such interruption in design is obvious. Often, however, the winding holes of conversions were cut carelessly (for example they may not be truly circular) and this can be a good guide. Matted centres tend to be mostly pre-1750 (though they persist later in the south) and as clock movement pillars before 1750 are often turned and finned, the absence of this turning and finning may help in spotting a newer movement.

147

Before getting further into recognition features, let us consider some of the other reasons behind conversions. I outlined one relatively innocent type of conversion. A more sinister type of movement-switching is done today by a considerable number of antique dealers, who regularly make 30-hour brass dial clocks into 8-day ones. This is done to cater for the high public demand for 8-day clocks and to meet this modern reversal of tastes of former times, dealers are obligingly at work to turn the commoner 30-hour clocks into the less-common 8-day types. One could censure such dealers, though one cannot altogether blame the restorers, who are merely taking on the work that is brought them. One could equally blame the public, who in many cases will buy a faked 8-day clock in preference to a genuine 30-hour, just for the ease of a once-a-week winding. Fortunately for those who wish to discriminate these modern conversion jobs are usually almost as easy to spot as the older ones.

Another type of conversion is done by the handyman, who likes to dabble with clocks. He is not a dealer, but buys clocks now and then, messes about with them, and then advertises them for sale privately—and of course avoids being taxed on his profits. This type is often the worst of all and the conversions can usually be detected by a child, yet people still continue to buy these clocks. Conversions that I have seen include brass 'dials', which were merely plain sheets of brass riveted on top of a painted dial with black numbering and a name painted onto the brass. I have seen such clocks with movements operating on solder, bits of string, plastic wire and pieces of Meccano (literally)—absolute horrors, yet eventually some bargain hunter buys them.

What do we look for to detect modern, and sometimes older, conversions? In case anyone is in doubt, clockmakers never made brass dial clocks where the brass dial was riveted over a painted dial, nor brass dials on to which the numbers were painted—they were *always* engraved. Switched movements can usually be spotted by taking a quick look behind the dial. A 'wrong' movement would almost always have needed some alteration to its method of attaching to the dial. On brass dial clocks the dial attached by three or four 'dial feet', which were fixed onto the dial and project through the movement frontplate, fastening inside the movement by means of pins. A movement from a different clock would almost certainly have its holes for these dial feet in the wrong positions. A faker faced with this situation has two alternatives.

The easiest, and the one most commonly taken, was simply to drill three (or four) new holes in the movement frontplate and pin the dial feet through these new holes. This means that three or four (sometimes fewer) original holes are now left spare, and it should be obvious at a glance that such spare holes in a frontplate, *serving no purpose*, are indications of where a previous dial was fitted. Sometimes a faker can use one or even two of the original holes, and this might mean only one or two left spare. Sometimes a new hole may run into an old one, but it should not be too hard to spot, and one or more spare dial feet holes almost always means that a faker has been at work. Some fakers, aware that purchasers may sometimes look out for empty holes, take the trouble to fill up any that would give the game away, by cutting a piece of brass to the right size and hammering it in to fill the spare hole. This can usually be detected as the brass filling may be different in colour or grain from the rest of the frontplate.

The alternative approach is to make use of existing frontplate holes by moving the dial feet into positions where they will mate up with them. This involves sawing off the dial feet and fitting new ones in the required positions, and leaves either tell-tale stumps showing the saw-marks, or else less obvious traces where these stumps have been filed level. If you look however, signs of the faker are always there.

Another point to watch for on a conversion from 30-hour to 8-day is the existence or otherwise of a seconds dial. Original 8-day clocks almost always have a seconds dial, though not in absolutely every instance. An 8-day clock without a seconds dial is exceptionally unusual and deserves a close look for that very reason. Thirty-hour clocks very rarely have a seconds dial. Most converted 30-hour clocks now having 8-day movements do not have seconds dials, simply because the original (30-hour) dial was not designed to show seconds and the faker seldom takes the trouble to make a seconds dial for it; engraving a new seconds dial involves a degree of skill which most fakers do not possess, and few have old seconds dial rings available. This means that if your suspicions are aroused by the absence of a seconds dial, and you glance at the movement, looking especially at the part immediately behind the place where the seconds dial would normally be

A print of 1748 showing a watchmaker at work—*see* Notes on the
Clocks Illustrated

(just below XII), you might very easily see the extended arbor onto which
the second hand was intended to fit—if, that is, the movement is a switched
one from some other 8-day clock. You might also look to see if such an ex-
tension arbor has been chopped off to camouflage this tell-tale inconsis-
tency. A seconds hand arbor on the movement with no seconds feature on
the dial, often tells you that movement and dial do not belong together
(there are rare exceptions to this, as to almost all these rules).

Other sub-dials can serve as a guide in just the same way. A dial from a
30-hour clock (now posing as an 8-day) may have a calendar indicator or
moon dial. Look to see if these work, and if they do not work, then a glance
should indicate whether any connecting work ever has moved them. The

driving system for calendar indicators on 8-day and 30-hour clocks are usually quite different, and without going into technical details, it is often obvious that a switched 8-day movement has no means of driving sub-dials on a dial to which it did not originally belong.

The winding squares on a converted clock may not be centrally placed in the (newly cut) winding holes. The squares themselves may protrude beyond the dial, being too long, or may be too short and unduly recessed behind the dial. An iron falseplate attached behind a *brass* dial is an indication of a fake. Falseplates were sold with *painted* dials, by the dialmakers. Fortunately the names on many falseplates can be checked against lists of known painted dialmakers for period.

Conversion is usually of two kinds: either 8-day brass dial clocks from 30-hour ones, or 30-hour brass dial clocks from 30-hour painted dial ones, and many of the points already mentioned will be equally valid in helping to recognise this latter type. Few people yet bother to convert 30-hour painted dial clocks into 8-day painted dial ones, though I have seen a few of this sort, and no doubt it will become common practice before long.

The other kind of fake not yet discussed, is the clock made up from genuine old bits and pieces. Here the field is wide open for the enthusiastic dabbler who has a pile of old spares. Oddly enough most of the fakes of this type seem to have been made by men who had never seen a real clock in its entirety. If you gave a dismantled bicycle to an Amazonian headhunter he might make something very wonderful from it, but it is unlikely that it would be a bicycle as we know it. Many of these fakes seem to have been made by horological Amazonian bicycle-makers. Guidance at spotting this type can only be vague, but experience and ordinary observation will normally allow you to spot one without difficulty. The presence of 1670 cherub-head spandrels and 1850 brass hands, attached to a 1790 painted dial with single-handed 1730 brass chapter ring and a 1770 Father Time swinging his scythe drunkenly across a moon dial arch at highwater time, whilst Adam and Eve lurch back and forth to avoid being reaped when the clock strikes . . . such confusion would strike even a beginner immediately, quite apart from the fact that it bears the name of Thomas Tompion!

There is one area, however, where such fakes are found not infrequently and that is in grandmother clocks. In the minds of many people this term conjures up a picture of a mini-grand'father clock, that is a smaller, neater, more easily accommodated 'pocket' grandfather—and so they are, in a way. The only trouble is that grandmother (some call them grand-daughter) clocks are either fakes or modern. Modern ones seem to start about 1860 or 1870 and were made into the 1920s (and still are made today, of course). Some of these are superb little examples made in the traditional manner but with all the most sought-after features, ie small height, narrow case, choice wood and so on, not strictly antique, yet highly desirable items and easily saleable. Most grandmother clocks come into a different category however.

I am given to understand that there *are* a few original miniature clocks by, for example, Edward East. Such clocks, however, are so rare that they number a mere handful and are mostly in museums. This does not deter many owners of grandmother clocks from feeling that theirs is one of the genuine ones.

There is even some doubt as to what constitutes a grandmother. Some books suggest that a grandfather of less than 6ft 6in is a grandmother, in which case I have handled very many such clocks and many ordinary country cottage grandfathers with square dials would qualify. This is not a fair classification. A true grandmother would probably stand no higher than 6ft, maybe 5ft 6in even, and have a dial maybe 6–8in square. It is not just the height but the overall proportions and dial size which matter. Essentially it is unimportant at what point one makes the division, since whilst small grandfathers may well be genuine (or larger ones that have been cut down), real grandmothers are so very rare that those met with are virtually certain to be fakes—except for the modern ones already described.

It is difficult to convince people of something they do not wish to believe. I am sure that many people who own a grandmother clock will decide that theirs is one of the very special rare exceptions which is quite genuine. I can remember once going to a house to buy a few clocks and spare parts which had been the property of a clock restorer who had recently died. There were various half-converted clocks, 30-hour dials drilled ready for 8-day movements, a pile of left-over 30-hour movements without dials, and various bits and pieces, but there was not a genuine clock in the house. There were, however, three superb grandmother cases, about 5ft 6in tall;

slim, neat, mellow, original-looking woods, one even had superb shell and urn inlays and tiny swan-necked pediments . . . unfortunately the untimely death of the restorer had left them unfinished. Woods and shell-inlays had been taken from original cases of ordinary size. Cases of this nature, cleverly finished and with twenty or thirty years of polishing, would fool a lot of people, and of course, because of their diminutive size, grandmother clocks fetch relatively high prices. A good modern cabinetmaker can produce 'antique' items that would deceive even most dealers. I saw one such recently in a beautifully neat mahogany case, standing about 6ft high. This is rather an interesting story as, quite by chance I came across the last three successive owners. The case was beautiful, but in my opinion Edwardian at the oldest, an old miniature reproduction of a late eighteenth-century style. The clock it housed was an obvious fake being a converted 30-hour, now 8-day, with the winding holes wrongly cut right into the pattern. Owner one bought this clock having had an acquaintance first 'vet' it for him. Having got the clock home to a restorer for cleaning, it was found that the movement had been switched—although this would have been obvious from the outset to someone with a little knowledge. Owner one therefore sold the clock to owner two, a dealer in whose shop I saw it. It was so obviously faked that I did not ask the price. A few weeks later I saw it again, this time in the shop of owner three, another dealer. It is amusing how you sometimes follow items around in this way, running into them in different shops, and watching the price rise all the time. Anyway, this particular clock when I last saw it had reached £450. It was worth maybe £50, if, that is, anyone wanted a desirably neat £50 1750 30-hour clock, converted to an 8-day with later repro case. There are other identification features about this clock, which I avoid giving to save red faces. Some dealers use the term 'furnishing piece' to describe such a desirable item but it is really a simple fake and should be recognised as such.

One reason that I give these recognition tips is that eventually the public at large may know enough and care enough to be able to recognise such fakes, and once this happens the bottom will drop right out of the fakes market. Nobody wants to own a clock which all his friends will recognise as a fake; at present, if only the owner knows, it does not seem to matter all that much. I find it most distressing that a genuine 30-hour country clock will often realise far less than a slick concoction of old clock scraps in a mini mahogany case.

Let us return, however, to the subject of dials and to the ways of recognising fakes. Many, particularly grandmother dials, are made from old bits and pieces and are sometimes 8 or 9in wide, although they may be as small as 6in. The dials are usually square, less often arched. An arched dial has disadvantages for the faker because there is more dial to fake and it puts the height up by 3in or more—hence arched dial fakes are fewer. Still, be on your guard against them, since a faker may be aware that, being fewer in number, arched dials fetch more money than square ones.

Let us consider the problems facing the maker of fake miniature dials. Whilst many have been made for financial gain, some of the older ones were no doubt made by clockmakers or apprentices as a kind of exercise or for fun even, using up old cast-off parts. This might give a wily dealer the opportunity to pass off such a fake as an 'apprentice-piece', which may sound like a highly desirable item. In my view a fake is a fair description for something which has been made to look like something it isn't, and our best guide in recognising one lies in the fact that the faker does not readily have the right parts for the job, and therefore uses whatever is to hand that will most nearly do the job. These small grandmother dials are a real headache to him, as there are no real small parts available and his choice is therefore very limited.

The dial sheet can be a real dial sheet cut down to size, or can be a new sheet of brass. A glance behind such a dial may show spare holes, where former spandrels fitted, signs of where the original dial feet were sawn off, or, if of the northern pierced dial plate type (with 'cartwheel' centre), it may be an obviously poor fit for the present chapter ring. Sometimes a real dial centre may be used (cut down at the edges) where that dial centre is of the type with an engraved maker's name on it. Signatures are difficult to obtain and a 'genuine' signature of this sort would never be passed up. The fitting of a standard 8-day longcase movement (usually of early to mid-nineteenth-century make) onto such a dial almost always means that the winding holes are disproportionately widely spaced apart for the size of dial, and sometimes so wide apart that they cut right through the chapter ring—an extremely suspicious sign on any provincial longcase clock. Just as when converting 30-hour clocks to 8-day ones, the making up of clocks from old bits involves problems over the seconds dial. Simply for convenience such fakes seldom have them—again a suspicious sign. If they do have them then they are often old seconds chapter rings from standard-sized clocks, and are therefore disproportionately large for a grandmother.

The chapter ring itself will quite probably be a real one from an old lantern clock. As these are normally one-handers, marked on their inner edge with quarter-hour divisions and half-hour fleur-de-lis-type markers, it usually means that the faker has to buzz minutes around the outer edge with a drill, making 'dotted minutes'. Apart from the anachronistic crudity of engraving style on the lantern clock chapter ring, it is also an incongruity to have quarter-hour and half-hour markers at the same time as dotted minutes. Minutes marked by dots are almost always *after* the quarter- and half-hour markers have been dropped. In other words, making a late seventeenth-century or early eighteenth-century lantern chapter ring look like a late eighteenth-century 8-day grandmother one, is an operation which is doomed before it begins—to those who will bother to look at the details.

Sometimes, a new chapter ring is made purposely, though not often, as the essence of these fakes in the past was to make them from available junk, rather than to actually go to expense in making them from scratch. The future trends of course may not be the same, as prices are rising very rapidly. A new chapter ring (made up say, fifty years ago) can usually be recognised by its engraving, although this requires a basic experience which only familiarity with real clocks will bring.

Spandrels are also a problem on grandmother dials, as most ordinary spandrels would be far too large for the dial size. The solution most often used is to take either original or reproduction spandrels of the small winged cherub-head type, as used on late seventeenth-century London longcase clocks. This type of spandrel is, of course, totally out of keeping with clocks of the late eighteenth century, which seems to be the most favoured period for the grandmother.

Signatures of made-up clocks have always posed a problem—hence the majority of fakes don't have one. A nameless original clock is unusual, almost a scarcity, since makers were obliged to sign their work by law, and also, of course, they would wish to advertise their skills by a prominent display of their name. This means that *any* nameless brass dial clock should put you immediately on the alert. A square dial clock without a name may, perhaps, have once been an arched dial with name in the arch. Rather than repair a badly damaged arch someone may have thought it simplest to chop off the arch altogether, throw out the surplus bit with the name on, and there you have a neat square dial clock, 'unsigned'. Faked signatures are often detectable by the very inferior quality of engraving in the name compared to the rest of the dial. Often faked signatures are in Victorian 'copperplate' script, very different in lettering style from eighteenth-century script.

Nothing is quite as helpful in detecting a fake as a knowledge of, and familiarity with, the real thing. At a recent antiques fair I saw a large veneered case of about 1850 (what some books might call a Yorkshire clock) containing a brass dial made-up fake. It was obvious that this case was made in 1840 or 1850 for a painted dial clock. It could not possibly have been made for any other kind of clock and therefore a brass dial in it was instantly and obviously 'wrong'. There was no need even to look closely at the dial, which was a virtually impossible (for a *brass* dial) 15in wide! The obvious fake was nearly £300.

Genuine musical or chiming clocks are very scarce. They have a third train, that is, an additional barrel and weight and winding hole in the dial to operate the musical system. Musical clocks are virtually always 8-day ones (I know there are very rare exceptions which run for thirty hours, but these are so rare the reader will probably never see one). Three-train clocks are often fakes and a three-train clock therefore merits much closer than average inspection, especially of the third (musical) train. Very often the third train was added later in Victorian times, perhaps when there was a craze for musical boxes and musical toys. The Victorians do get blamed for all manner of crimes—in clocks this is mostly because they were guilty!

An original three-train clock was planned that way, and from the point of view of appearance the winding holes were almost always symmetrically placed. Where the third train has been added later, this has usually involved bolting a musical train onto the movement at some convenient spot. The result is that often the winding square has met the dial at some comic position, such as through a number on the chapter ring. A glance inside may reveal that the musical train is an obvious later attachment. Sometimes the tune(s) played may give a clue to the date of the musical train. The common West-minster chimes are, of course, Victorian. One musical clock which I saw recently in a dismantled state during cleaning (made by William Coulson of York) had engraved on an inner plate 'musical train made by W. Newey, York' followed by a mid-nineteenth-century date. Most fakers are not so obligingly honest. The clock, of course, was more than a century older than the musical train.

I remember once viewing a clock by a Plymouth maker with a view to buying it, an 8-day, brass dial with arched moonwork in a very fine and mellow mahogany case. Such little experience as I then had was almost exclusively with northern clocks, since, whilst northern clocks drift southwards over the years, southern ones very rarely wander northwards. This clock in question was a fine example and I would have been pleased to buy it, but one thing disturbed me. Visible on the front of the one-piece silvered dial were four screwheads, which proved to be holding the dial feet. This, I was sure, was evidence of faking, for who in his right mind would make a beautifully engraved dial only to marr it by four screwheads? No one, I decided, and I dismissed it as a fake. Since then I have learned that this very shoddy practice, to my knowledge unknown in the north, was not at all uncommon in the south, including London. The point of this story is not to point out the (acknowledged) superiority of northern clockmakers over their southern contemporaries, but to show that the person who looks hard enough may find fakes where none exist.

So far we have considered almost exclusively clocks with brass dials. Those with painted dials have been much less subject to faking in the past, largely because of their lower commercial value. White dial clocks have not been worth faking; they have been plundered for use in faking brass dial ones. Quite a few original musical clocks have had their original white dials swopped for brass ones in an attempt to make them into more desirable fakes. But there is still very much more likelihood that a white dial clock will be in its original state, unbutchered by fakers and dabblers.

I have tried to leave out altogether technical aspects concerned with the actual construction of clocks, except such aspects as are easily understood by all. Those for whom this technical side is interesting will find much useful information in some of the books listed in the bibliography. However, I find that the vast majority of readers do not wish to become mechanical engineers, but do appreciate guidance from *visible* evidence, such as dial features. Recognition from visible features means that a prospective customer can assess a clock in a shop without having to ask to be shown interior features, although it is always advisable to check the movement before finally deciding to buy. No genuine dealer will object to showing the movement, in fact he will probably be pleased that the customer takes so much interest. Buying a clock is something that most people do only once; as in marriage, if you choose in haste, you may very well find yourself repenting at leisure.

We have still to consider fake cases. Fortunately these are extremely rare, with the exception of grandmother cases, which were obviously made up to suit faked grandmother clocks. Miniature modern cases are still made today, but these are generally recognisable as being brand new. There are a few cases, though only a few, which were newly constructed perhaps fifty years ago to house clocks whose cases had suffered serious damage or deterioration. Whilst these cases were made in traditional style, the makers seldom had more than a vague idea of the shape and virtually no conception of the features of the relevant period. Such cases therefore, usually in oak, look rather 1920ish, were originally French polished (which after fifty years usually goes off and leaves the white grain filler showing), and no one could be deceived into thinking that they were anything other than old replacements. Of course, they were never intended to deceive.

The reason for the lack of faked cases is again financial; provincial clocks were just not valuable enough. Today, this situation is changing rapidly and we can now expect faked cases to begin to be made, especially in view of the fact that clocks survive in far greater numbers than their cases. Any dealer will tell you that it is by no means unusual to buy a clock without a case, but to come by a case without a clock is quite uncommon. Hence dealers ultimately acquire more clocks than cases. The time has come when we are going to have to start to have new cases made to house such clocks. New cases made for this purpose would need to copy as accurately as possible the appropriate style, but they should be seen as modern replacements not as fakes.

Only in one area is there any serious difficulty over cases and this is when

cases have been swopped and changed between clocks. As has been explained, the clock and case were normally bought separately and the complete clock was therefore, from its very beginning, a marriage of two
distinct parts. Because of this it is often argued that it is no great detriment to
a clock that it has a different case from that with which it started life. That
argument may be voiced all the more strongly by a dealer who is trying to
sell a clock in a replacement case. It is to some extent a matter of individual
opinion. However, there must unquestionably be more merit in a clock and
case which are original to each other, than in one where the case can be seen
to be a replacement. At the same time a replacement case need not be considered a terrible tragedy provided it is of the right sort, that is, of compati-
ble age and style with the clock (and, if need be, of the right regional
variation). The whole problem of case-swopping revolves around the question of whether the person who did that swopping, had the knowledge to
put a case of the correct type around the clock—and most had not!

A few tips are given here which may assist in recognising a replacement
case. They are, however, only tips, not inflexible rules, and whilst each one
may be a pointer towards a case being 'wrong' for the clock, there are
exceptional circumstances which could explain its presence on a 'right' case.
It should be superfluous to say that by far the best way of recognising a
'wrong' case is to study as many clocks as possible until you are familiar
with the styles of different periods and regions. The extent of the experience
to be gained by the enthusiast will naturally be limited by the time at his dis-
posal for such study and examination of clocks. With all due respect to 'collectors', the average dealer is likely to handle and examine far more clocks
in a year than the average collector does in several. It follows that in talking
with dealers some of their experience may rub off, although it must be said
that few dealers like their showrooms to be used as free museums or particularly enjoy giving conducted tours around them.

Supposing that the case style is roughly acceptable to the clock—what
points are worth checking? It would be as well to see that the dial size fits the
hood aperture, as clockmakers seldom used cases for their clocks where the
hood aperture was a different size from the dial. The hood aperture on most
clocks is not the same thing as the hood door, nor always the same size as it.
The hood aperture is the interior framing surrounding the dial, visible

when the hood door is open (some are just visible when the hood door is closed). This interior framing will usually be fractionally smaller than the dial size, for example a 13in-wide dial might fit behind a 12½in or 12¾in aperture, giving just a little overlap to avoid gaps at the dial edges. Sometimes the interior framing could be appreciably smaller than the hood door aperture: a 12in glazed area on a door might sometimes have an 11in aperture to the interior framing. A difference between the size of the inner framing and glass area need not indicate tampering, though it could do, and it is probably worth a second glance. I have seen brass dials with strips of brass added around their edges to make a 10in dial fit an 11in case, these added strips being obvious fake additions. (A more commonsense approach might have led the faker to add ½in beading around the inner edge of the hood aperture.) When considering whether the dial 'fits' the case then, one must look at both dial *and* inner hood opening for signs of tampering.

The seatboard and its supports often show signs of more recent sawing or shaping where a clock has been put into a wrong case. At the same time old seatboards (often of softwood) do frequently suffer from woodworm and can be legitimate replacements on the right case. I myself have often had to replace wormy seatboards.

If you examine the path of descent of the weight(s) you may notice grooves or slight scuffing marks on the inner case framework, caused by the weight(s) rubbing when descending. The signs of one such mark centrally on a case now containing a two-weighted clock, suggest that it may have originally been the case of a 30-hour clock. The converse also applies of course. Similarly if the weight(s) now rub at different points from those where the old rubbing marks are, this again suggests the case may not be the correct one for the clock. However, this could be caused by the weights themselves being replacements, or by a new seatboard, and/or new gutlines hanging from different suspension points—in other words these factors alone are not damning evidence.

Most cases have scratchmarks on the inner backboard, where the pendulum adjustion nut has bumped or scraped against it at times when the clock was leaning too far backwards. A different clock in that case may have a slightly different pendulum length, pendulum bob, adjustion nut, or arc of swing, and may therefore not rub consistently with old scratchmarks on the backboard. Again this is not totally damning, since a pendulum might be a legitimate replacement for a damaged one (on the original clock).

Another pointer is that 30-hour cases would usually have a turnbuckle catch, and 8-day ones a lock. One would not normally have wished to lock and unlock a clock case every single day when winding, though the existence of some 30-hour cases with apparently original locks suggests that people occasionally did wish to lock up daily.

Commonsense is worth applying. One would not normally expect a 30-hour cottage clock to have a high-quality 'mansion' case, nor would one expect a superb 8-day clock of above-average quality to have a painted soft-wood case. The man who could afford a good clock could afford a case worthy of it.

Restoration of casework is to be expected in some degree. The commonest place to look for this is at the base of the clock. Feet or plinths are frequently replacements and sometimes the entire base is replaced up to, and including, the mouldings attaching it to the trunk. An oak case with cross-banding in walnut to the hood door and trunk, would hardly have been made with a plain base panel, nor even a base panel cross-banded in mahogany. Cross-banding is often patched with wrong wood, either through ignorance or unavailability of the right wood. Base panels would have had that cross-banding on all four edges. Banding on the top and sides of a base panel and *not* along the lower edge, is almost always a sign of a cut-down base, or replacement feet/plinth, or both.

This type of base restoration is not terrible. It is to be expected to some extent on very old clocks, and whilst not exactly desirable, it need not be enormously detrimental. One has to expect and accept a certain amount of wear and tear. All the same you ought to be able to spot such restoration, you might not object to it, provided you know it's there. The customer who buys a clock without noticing this type of restoration until he gets the clock home, may find he then loses some of his regard for it and for his own judgement too—at least the latter *should* apply.

Dealers too make mistakes, and they can be costly ones. I recall a sale not long ago where a clock was sold for about £300. A few weeks later it was back again in the same saleroom and this time was sold for considerably less.

The dealer who had bought it had discovered his mistake too late and had put the clock back into the sale again, cutting his losses. In a way this was an honourable thing to do—many would have sold it in their shops and hoped the next buyer was also taken in by it. This is a point worth remembering. If a clock appears to go cheaply at a sale, it is very unlikely to be a lucky accident. Most sales are viewed by a whole army of dealers and their combined skills don't miss much. If nobody wants to bid you can assume there is a good reason, and if you want a 'duff' clock, one way to get one is to pick up a 'bargain' at a sale. By all means pit your wits against the trade at a sale—if you have the expertise to do so, but if you jump in at the deep end without this expertise, you have only yourself to blame if you drown. In the end you usually get what you pay for. I hope some of the above points may save the less-experienced a few grey hairs.

The unfortunate, who does buy a pig in a poke, may take comfort in the following few lines from a letter written in 1816 by Henry Ecroyd to Henry Spencer, a watchmaker at Burnley, Lancashire—a customer who, though disappointed, had by no means lost his sense of humour:

Friend, I have sent thee my pocket companion which greatly stands in need of thy kind care and correction. The last time he was at thy school he was no ways benefitted by thy discipline—nor in the least reformed thereby. When thou layest thy chastening hand upon him, let it be without passion, lest in thine anger thou drive him to distraction. I perceive by the index of his mind he is a liar, and that his motions are wavering and irregular, his pulse too beats sometimes very quick which betokens him not of an even temper, at other times he worketh so sluggish notwithstanding.

I frequently urge him that when he should be upon his watch (as thou knoweth his usual name denoteth) I find him slumbering and sleeping, or as the vanity of human wisdom would phrase it, I catch him napping: hence I am induced to believe he is not right in his inner man. Examine him therefore, I beseech thee, and prove him, by being well acquainted with his inward frame and disposition, drive him from the error of his ways and show him the path wherein he should go. It grieveth me to think, and when I ponder thereupon I am verily of opinion his body is foul, purge him therefore with thy cleansing instrument from all pollution and prove him according to truth. I'll place him under thy care for a few days and pay for his board when thou requireth it. In thy last bill thou charged me with the eighth part of a pound sterling which I will most assuredly pay when thy work deserveth it. Do thou regulate his conduct for the time to come by the motion of the luminary that rules over the day, and let him learn of that unerring guide the true calculation of his table and the equation of time, and when thou finds him converted from the error of his ways and conformable to the above mentioned rules, do thou send him with a true bill of charge drawn in the spirit of moderation, and it shall be faithfully remitted to thee by thy true friend, on the second day of the week commonly called Monday . . .

NOTES ON THE CLOCKS
ILLUSTRATED

Thomas Loomes At The Mermayd In Lothbury (p 20)
This is a typical lantern clock by Thomas Loomes, who was free of the
Clockmakers' Company in 1649. The clock was made originally with balance-wheel control, as all his clocks probably were, and was later converted
to short pendulum. This allows us to date its construction quite accurately as
being between 1649 and 1658, after which he would have built his clocks on
the pendulum principle, if indeed he still continued to produce clocks under
his own name which, in view of his connection with Fromanteel, is very
doubtful. It measures 13 × 6½in at the widest points. The bell is supported by
an internal iron stand as opposed to the more normal bell straps. As this type
of bell support is also known on some Fromanteel lantern clocks, and as
Thomas Loomes married the elder Fromanteel's daughter in 1654, that may
suggest that this clock dates between 1654 and 1658.

It is an alarm clock, the central disc being used to set the alarm. Notice the
blank shield on the fret, probably left blank for the coat of arms of the
owner to be inserted. This is a 'Cromwellian' clock in more ways than one,
though that expression is frowned upon in horological circles. The photograph omits the finial at the top of the bell, as it is a modern replacement.

Johannes Shepley (p 91 and 127)
An early 30-hour clock of about 1710. It has a single-handed 10in square dial
which is in many ways typical, and stylistically this clock could date any-
where between 1690 and 1720. A maker of the same name died in Stock-
port, Cheshire in 1750, and he is assumed to be the same person. Latinisation

of the name (John to Johannes) is often a sign of an early date, though not all makers did this (compare *John* Williamson) and some names did not lend well to Latinising, eg Thomas and Robert. The case is of plain oak, blackened, with a pierced fret above the dial, a canopy to the hood, lenticle glass to the door—in many ways an archetypal case, the outline of which continued with only minor modifications for many years. The case of the Woolley clock is very similar (p 127). The Shepley case stands about 6ft 3in. The dial has a solid dial sheet, not the usual cut-away northern type.

A. Fromanteel Londini fecit (p 33)
A beautiful 8-day Fromanteel dial, though not one of his earliest, as this one was made about 1680 or a little later. The dial has the typical London cherub-head spandrels, finely matted dial centre and very small minute numbers. The ringing around the winding holes is not usually found before about 1680; its purpose is said to have been to prevent scratchmarks on the matting from careless insertions of the key.

The hands are especially fine. They are far more ornate at this time than on his earlier clocks (compare the Thomas Loomes lantern clock hand of about thirty years earlier). These hands are amongst the finest ever made and one would not expect the hands of later provincial clocks to compare with them.

John Williamson in Leeds fecit (p 92 and 93)
This is a superb example of an early provincial clock showing how these followed on from London inspiration. This man was a London clockmaker, free of the Clockmakers' Company in 1682, but almost at once he moved to Leeds where he married in 1683 and spent the rest of his life. Coming as he did straight from London, it is not surprising that his style is the London style. This clock dial is similar in many ways to the Fromanteel clock on p 33, although this one is a rare month clock and was made about 1690–1700. It has the London style cherub-head spandrels. The case would almost certainly have come from London, being an elaborate and costly marquetry one (with replacement feet). Notice the cresting of the hood is a cherubs and crown theme, reminiscent of the twin-cherub spandrel pattern found about this same period. The hour hand is of very fine workmanship, but the minute hand is a much later replacement. The engraved circular area

around the hands pipe is a feature which appeared for a short period about this time. A little engraving between the spandrels is also an early sign. This is obviously amongst the finest of early provincial work, although I have not seen the movement.

An illustration of the peaks to which provincial makers could rise (if they could find customers wealthy enough) may be seen from a recently discovered clock by this maker, which runs for a year at one winding. That in itself is a rarity but the clock in question, in addition to striking the hours, also has a ting-tang pull quarter-repeat mechanism, ie it will indicate the quarter-hour by the ting-tang bell system whenever the repeater cord is pulled. A tremendous store of power is required to drive such a clock for a year, this being done by skillful gearing of the wheel trains. A mystery as yet unsolved is how a man of such ability came to end his days in the workhouse, which was where Williamson died in 1747.

John Smallwood: Chelford (p 94)
This is a fine quality 8-day clock probably made about 1700. The movement has finned pillars and rack striking. The spandrels are well finished. Though they are a tight fit on this dial (which is only 10in square) this often happens where this spandrel pattern is used on a small dial and they are believed to be original. The half-hour marker is of an interesting early style, but notice a slip of the engraving tool on the one directly above Chelford. The engraving is deep and clear. The date box is circular and ringed to make it match the winding holes. The winding squares are filed into flower heads, like four-leaved clovers, a nice touch showing that the maker took that little extra trouble. Both hands are believed to be original, the hour hand being especially fine. The maker is believed to have been the same man as John Smallwood of Macclesfield (Cheshire) who died in 1715.

Wolley—Codnor (see p 168 and 127)
This is a good 8-day clock made about 1740–50 by James Woolley of Codnor, Derbyshire, who usually signed his clocks Wolley. The 12in square dial is cut away behind the chapter ring in typical northern style (it is probably more correct to say 'cast away'). The movement is unusual in several ways, most of which are indicative of its high quality. It has five pillars instead of the normal four. The tails of the steel parts are finished in a decor-

Eight-day clock by Wolley of Codnor, c1745

ative manner. It has a repeater of the more complex type worked by a star-wheel—the repeater cord passes over an apparently original upright pulley on the seatboard and runs through a hole in the trunk moulding just above the door, where it is held in place by a small button. The small spandrels each side of the seconds dial are unusual (compare with plate on p 95). The hands are of fine quality and apparently original. The calendar is unusual in having a separate small chapter ring and in being indicated by a pointer—pointer calendars usually date from much later in the century. The case is of plain blackened oak standing about 7ft high. Note the pierced fret above the dial, shaped hood canopy, and lenticle glass.

The maker was an exceptionally interesting character of an eccentric nature. He was born about 1700 and died in 1786, being succeeded at clock-making by his nephew, John Woolley, who survived his uncle by only nine years. James Woolley's clocks seem to be of a much better than average quality. The earliest reference to this maker (supplied by Mr N. Bestwick) comes from a Lincolnshire farmer's diary: '1724, July 10th. Bot at Derby Market from Wolley of Codnor, square oak clock. Paid £4. 10s. He wanted £5.' This seems to confirm that such clocks were taken to market to sell, and sometimes, as here, in cases. This must have been an oak-cased 30-hour one, which we might expect to have been normally priced about £2 10s plus £1 10s for the case, making £4. The fact that Woolley could ask £5 and get £4 10s must mean it was above average in quality. (It is too cheap to have been an 8-day clock.)

Woolley's eccentric nature made him a legend in his own lifetime. His determination to succeed made him a tireless worker and this, coupled with an economy which made him almost a miser, eventually amassed him a fortune. It is told how, even when a wealthy man, he trod barefoot through the dewy fields carrying his shoes and stockings in his hand to avoid wetting them. On one occasion he decided that plough horses were too costly to maintain for the small benefit they yielded. Consequently he sold them and when ploughing time came round he hired a group of labourers to pull the plough. Their efforts, however, were costly in food and drink and nowhere near comparable to those of horses. To make matters worse crowds of people gathered from miles around to witness this unusual spectacle. An old account of the incident continues

he tried, but in vain, to keep them off; they thronged upon him from all quarters; his gates were all set open or thrown off their hinges; and the fences broken down in every direction. Woolley percieved his error; the men, the rope traces, and the plough were all sent home in a hurry, and with some blustering and many oaths, the trespassers were got rid of.

He is another example of a provincial clockmaker who tried to do things in his own way, if not always successfully!

Burges de Wigan (p 95 and 96)
This is an early 8-day clock of good quality. The arch is a separate piece of the dial, added to the square, though apparently a contemporary addition and carefully made to match the square in having a double engraved border around it identical to that round the square. The moonwork, here showing a three-quarter moon, is of the engraved and silvered disc type, but here is most unusually positioned above the VI numeral. This was probably done in order to permit a seconds dial below the XII, where this type of moonwork is usually placed. The calendar pointer is positioned in the arch, again a most unusual method of showing the date and found occasionally on London clocks of the early arched dial period (1720s). Perhaps clockmakers were still experimenting with what use to make of the new arched area.

The pillars are turned and finned. The strikework uses the older locking-wheel method, attached to the great wheel inside the plates. This system lingered in provincial 8-day work to a surprisingly late date (the 1750s) long after the rack striking system had been introduced. As this locking-wheel system had no apparent advantages over rack striking (in fact it had the disadvantage of occasionally needing to be reset in sequence if the clock ran down fully) one must assume that its retention was for reasons of economy in manufacture.

The engraved design around the winding squares is most unusual, and the two small spandrels by the seconds dial are also extremely unusual both in design and position. The engraving is deep and bold with an interesting flourish to the 1 on, for example, 10 and 15. It is altogether a most unusual clock by a maker who thought for himself and worked in the tradition of the above-average 'school' of Wigan makers. The hour hand is believed to be a replacement, the minute hand original. John Burges is known to have worked at Wigan, Lancashire, from 1712 till his death there in 1754 aged about 65. The clock was made about 1720–30. The 12in-wide dial has the dial sheet cut away behind the chapter ring.

The case is of oak with walnut cross-banding, neatly proportioned but in the simple style and materials of the period and stands about 6ft 8in high.

William Drury—Gainsborough (see p 171)
This is a good quality 8-day clock of about 1730–40. The maker is immorta-

Eight-day clock by William Drury, Gainsborough, c1735

lised, like so many others, by failing to appear in the standard lists and nothing is known about him. He may perhaps be connected with a family of London clockmakers of this name. It has many of the usual early features. The hands may be original. The arch spandrels are of a most unusual pattern (an urn supported by two eagles), which would match those in the plate on p 173, though there is no reason to suppose that they are anything but original on this dial. The dial is 11in wide and has no northern cut-outs behind the chapter ring.

It has some unusual features too. The arch is used to accommodate a day-of-the-week dial, the panel for each day having the representation of the appropriate zodiacal figure—in our illustration it shows 'Saterday'. You occasionally see this type of day-of-the-week dial on London clocks of the same period. Another unusual feature is also reminiscent of better London work—the movement has five pillars instead of the normal four. This was for additional strength and rigidity. A further unusual feature (in the provinces) is that the maker fastened the fifth pillar by a latch instead of the normal pin. The clockmaker, or cleaner, when assembling the clock can clip the plates together quickly by means of this latch (on the centre pillar) thereby leaving the hands free to tap home the pins in the other four corner pillars. Early London clocks, such as those by the Fromanteel, normally had latch fastening to all pillars, but on provincial work latches are extremely rare. This clock has locking-wheel striking on the barrel, between the plates.

Wm Porthouse—Penrith (p 98)
This is a very fine 30-hour clock given a superficial resemblance to an 8-day one by virtue of its ringed 'winding holes', which of course are purely decorative and not winding holes at all, and also by virtue of being of the more costly arched type with moonwork. The dial is superb, being beautifully engraved, especially the attractive 'herring-bone' engraved border. The moon is of the early type with a silvered brass moon disc. The spandrels are well finished. The hands are apparently original, the hour hand worn very thin, and the unusual fish-tails on the minute hand base may well have been intended to partner the dolphin arch spandrels. The maker was from a family that made clocks for several generations. He was born in 1706 and died in 1790, leaving three sons who also followed this trade. This clock dates from about 1730–40.

Storer—Derby (p 173)
This is a good early 8-day clock dating from about 1730–40. The hands are believed to be original (despite being overlength, according to some authorities). The dial centre is matted with engraving around the datebox, typical of this time, as are the ringed winding holes. The chapter ring engraving is bold and firm. It carries diamond-shaped half-quarter markers which had become extremely rare by 1740. The 12in-wide dial sheet has cut-away sections behind the chapter ring. The engraved eagle on the arch

Eight-day clock by Thomas Storer, Derby, c1735

boss carries in its talons the legend *Tempus Fugit*, belying those who suggest that this motto appears only on late clocks. The corner spandrels are of the two-eagles-and-urn type; those in the arch are dolphins. It is a good sturdy clock, which I wish I had never sold. The case was rock-hard oak. The maker is unmentioned in any of the standard reference works.

Seddon—Frodsham (p 110)
This is an 8-day clock by John Seddon of Frodsham, Cheshire, made about

173

the middle of the century, c1750–60. It has a finely matted centre and typical half-hour markers. It is a little unusual in having the nameplate and seconds dial recessed into the 12in dial sheet, which is cut away behind the chapter ring.

The striking system is also unusual, being of the older locking-wheel principle working on the main barrel between the movement plates, but in this instance operated by a pin-wheel instead of the more normal notched locking-wheel. Unusual systems of this sort show that the maker had his own idiosyncratic methods and that there is no question of the clock being made from stock 'factory' parts. The spandrels are of the four seasons pattern—spring top left, summer top right, autumn bottom right, winter bottom left. This type of spandrel is cast in the solid with hardly any of the usual piercings. The winding squares seem unusually thick and heavy for the size of the holes, a sign one might often regard with suspicion, but these are original and presumably further evidence of the maker's individual style.

I P—Asby (p 82)
The maker of this clock remains something of a mystery. He is thought to have been John Powley of Asby, Westmorland. Stylistically the clock dates from about 1750–60. Its half-hour markers are of late simplified form and it has string-of-pearls spandrels and the later type of lunette calendar. It is a 30-hour clock, of course, but its most interesting feature is that it has rack striking fitted purposely to enable it to be used as a repeater. Even more interesting is that the rack striking work on this clock is positioned *between* the plates instead of in front of the frontplate, as is the usual practice. The apparently original case is fitted with a pulley to carry the repeater cord. The hands seem to be original. The dial is 11in square. Notice the 'blind' fretwork to the hood, purely for decoration.

Thomas Lister (p 175 and 137)
This is a superb 30-hour clock by Thomas Lister the elder of Luddenden, near Halifax, Yorkshire. Everyone in Halifax knows where Luddenden is, despite the fact that one national authority on clocks was unable to locate its whereabouts and doubted whether such a place existed! Lister was born in 1717 at Keighley, served his apprenticeship under John Stancliffe at nearby

Thirty-hour clock by Thomas Lister, Halifax, c1760

Barkisland, and set up on his own about 1738, the year when he married Hannah Holroid, a Barkisland girl. His son, Thomas the younger, born 1745, ultimately became a more famous clockmaker. Thomas the elder worked alone till about 1765, after which father and son probably worked together in Halifax. He died in 1779.

This clock, like many of his, is signed without the place-name, though he did sign some with *Luddenden*; after about 1765 he signed them *Halifax*. His clocks are mostly 30-hour square dial ones, like those Stancliffe made, but rather better.

This clock was probably made about 1760 or a little earlier by the senior Lister. It is in immaculate condition. The case is in oak of a pale golden colour standing 6ft 8in high. The dial is 11in square, has castle gateway

spandrels, lunette calendar above the VI, Halifax silvered moon below the
XII. The movement is a conventional plate-framed one; the dial is cut away
behind the chapter ring. The hands, undoubtedly original, are made of brass
(though in a contemporary steel design), which was a favourite quirk of the
elder Lister. The engraving is deep, bold and confident. It is an exceptionally
fine example of good sensible 30-hour country clockwork in almost mint
condition, all the more remarkable in view of the rough usage such clocks
had to tolerate.

Will Snows 660 (p 72)
A typical 30-hour clock by Will Snow the elder, the brass dial being 11in
square and cut away behind the chapter ring. The string-of-pearl spandrels,
dotted minute markers, engraved centre decoration, lunette type of calendar dial and hands pattern all suggest a date of around 1775–80; the number,
660, backs this up.

The movement is one of his typical 'skeleton-plate' versions, Mark Two
with steel cock and pillars. The hands are believed to be original. Will
Snow was born in 1736 and died in 1795 at his farm at Padside near Pateley
Bridge, Yorkshire.

Saml Roberts–Llanvair 265 (p 85)
This 30-hour two-handed clock by Roberts has a 10in square dial. *Llanvair
265* was his serial number, indicating that the clock was made in 1767. It has
normal locking-wheel striking and apparently a trigger for putting the
clock back into strike sequence in the event of its running down completely.
The hands appear to be original. The spandrels are of a country type of
crowned cherub-head. The lunette date is typical of this period. The dial
centre is weakly matted onto which is engraved a scrollwork design, but the
quality of engraving is poor and a probable indication that Roberts did it
himself. Notice the scroll design ends in what could be taken for ringed
winding holes. The dial is cut away behind the chapter ring.

J Barber–Winster (p 70)
A 30-hour clock by Jonas Barber the younger of Winster (Westmorland), a
very good provincial clockmaker whose work has many features which are
both distinctive and indicative of the high standards he maintained, even on

the simple country cottage clocks that formed the bulk of his output. Familiarity with his clocks enables me to say in this instance that even the hands and the case are definitely original—something one can seldom state with absolute certainty.

Barber numbered his clocks on the movement frontplate. This one is numbered 682, altered to 683, which we are able to say from studying his numbering system works out at about the year 1764, very close in period to that by Samuel Roberts, and comparison between the two is interesting. The engraving (Barber's own work) and the hands are both far better than those on Roberts's clock. Barber often put those strange encroaching strands of seaweed onto his matted backgrounds.

Barber's dial is 12in wide and has the usual northern cut-outs behind the chapter ring. His movements are held together not by the normal method of four taper pins but by two pins alternated with two latches, a most unusual feature on provincial work of this time—indeed it is probably a unique combination. Other minor individual touches (such as the double-tailed single 5 numeral) enable one to recognise his work so plainly that, like Will Snow's clocks, one can identify a Barber movement even without its dial.

He was born about 1718 and died in 1802, the last of his line. The plain oak case stands 6ft 9in high and is in superb condition. The hood top is of a most unusual, though original, shape. A pattern of criss-cross decorative saw-cuts just below the hood is found on a number of Barber's cases about this time, which may indicate that he used one particular casemaker. Barber clocks rightly have a very high reputation in their own locality.

James Park—Kilmalcolm (p 102)
An attractive Scottish 8-day clock with 13in wide dial dating from about 1760. The name boss in the arch is a fairly common feature of this time. The dolphin arch spandrels are a bolder than normal version of this pattern. The corner spandrels, however, are a most unusual pattern combining a female head in an oval surround surmounted by an urn; the raised lip along the lower edge of each spandrel is also unusual. The chapter ring carries a wavy 'Dutch' minute band and this is echoed in the scalloped and recessed seconds dial. The minute numbers show individual engraver's flourishes especially

Eight-day clock by Lawrie, Carlisle, c1760

on the 3's and 5's. The dial centre is very beautifully worked. The background is not matted, as it might at first seem to be, but each mark is made with a ring-ended punch and so the background consists of hundreds of tiny circles. The finely engraved scroll designs trail through this patterned background. The winding holes interrupt this scrollwork design and thus provide an instance where the clockmaker has broken the general rule in cutting his winding holes through the design *after* engraving, rather than in forming the design around the holes. The movement appears to be completely original to the dial, but this method of breaking into the design by the winding holes is not good practice. The dial sheet is cut away behind the chapter ring and the movement, whilst well made, is of conventional design.

Lawrie—Carlisle (p 178 and 134)

A very fine example of a better-quality 8-day provincial clock. The movement has a repeater spring. The dial plate is cut away behind the 13in dial in typical northern fashion. The style of the dial with question mark spandrels, centre fully and beautifully engraved, typical painted moon disc, all are suggestive of the 1755–70 period. However, the movement is numbered (no 10) inside. Archibald Lawrie moved to Carlisle about 1748 and it might seem reasonable to place this as one of his earliest numbered clocks, though we do not yet know when he began numbering.

Both the engraved flower-head patterns around the winding holes, and the filing of the winding squares themselves into four-leaved clover patterns are indicative of fine quality work. The movement is conventional but very well finished. The lead weights are pear-shaped.

The case is a superb example of better-quality northern casework in a version of a design that was a standard one from about 1760–90; it might have come straight from the pattern-books of Gillows of Lancaster, the famous cabinet makers. It is in solid mahogany with fine facing veneers and cross-banding and stands 7ft 6in high.

J Thompson—Darlington (p 129)

This is a 30-hour white dial pine-cased clock of the later eighteenth century, dating from about 1780–90. We illustrate this one because it is typical of the largely white dial style of this period with the beginnings of a vignette scene in the arch and standard numbering and hands (probably original). The case is most interesting being of stripped pine. It is in exceptional condition and the most attractive break-arch top, complete with central wooden finial is slightly unusual. There should be another wooden finial above each pillar. The door top and the mouldings are typical. James Thompson had a shop in High Row, Darlington, where he died in 1825.

J C Elliott—Leeds (p 180)

This is an extremely late clock of about 1855, of the kind that older books used to think was a typical Yorkshire clock. Of course Yorkshire and Lan-

Hood and dial of clock by J C Elliott, Leeds, c1855

cashire were amongst the few areas still selling longcase clocks as late as this, as by now most counties had given in to the increasing competition from America and Europe. The last bastions of the north held out, though fighting a rearguard action. Clocks such as this one are the product of that struggle.

The clock (movement and dial) was by this time almost entirely a factory product. The dial, and probably the complete movement, would have been bought-in by Elliott (probably from Birmingham) and he would have done no more than assemble the parts. There is usually no falseplate fitting on these late clocks. In this sense, therefore, there is nothing admirable or desirable about it. The dial shows that unleashed Victorian exuberance, a riot of fussy decoration which was then so popular.

To me these are very sad clocks. This casework is beautifully made, exhibiting the highest standards of craftsmanship. Today, however, they are unpopular, being thought to be in very vulgar taste by our present-day stainless steel standards! They are also too tall and too wide for modern homes and are therefore very hard to sell today in Britain. At the time they were made, however, such cases were trying to outdo those that had gone before. The choicest veneers of mahogany and rosewood were used (just try to buy West Indian mahogany today!) and note how the case was cross-banded, twice, even treble-banded in parts. The workmanship in that marquetry panel below the hood depicting flowers and galloping horses, is every bit as good as that in the marquetry work of an early London clock, although, of course, it covers a far smaller area. All this exuberance and lavish extravagance and all the cost that went into the making of such exotic cases, all this did no more than help to delay the inevitable collapse of native British longcase clockmaking for a further ten years or so. For a short time they caught the popular imagination in the north, though not in the south, where Jerome's 15s American tickers heralded the disposable age.

Today, however, we are relieved if we can get a European dealer to buy them, for nobody in Britain seems to want them. A clock like this should be in a museum as a supreme example of its period, yet I don't know any museum that would even consider buying such a clock, even at a giveaway price. They are much more a part of our heritage than American shelf clocks or 'Vienna' regulators, or even sixteenth-century prototype clocks from Germany. They can be bought cheaply now, sometimes (like this example) in near mint condition.

John Stancliffe—Halifax (p 137)
This case, housing a clock by John Stancliffe of Halifax, Yorkshire, is of

thick heavy oak, deeply carved and stained black, as most carved cases were. I believe that the carving was done at the time the clock was made (about 1765) and that the case was original to the clock. Carved cases of blackened oak were certainly popular in the Halifax area and the Lanca-shire-Yorkshire Pennine border area. The door of this case is almost an inch thick and the deep carving has still pierced right through it at one point. A normal (uncarved) door might be of half-inch thick oak at this period, or even quarter-inch, but the thickness of construction was (in my opinion) purely because it was to be a carved case.

The hood pillars and trunk quarter-pillars have unusual deep grooves in them, you could hardly call it reeding. This would be very strange on an uncarved case. I bought this clock from a consultant who had bought it at auction about 1950 for £8, which is indicative of the public regard for such clocks at that time. Today its worth is more appreciated.

Dammant–Colchester (p 122)
This spring-driven table clock, usually called a bracket clock, was made about 1725 by Barnaby Dammant of Colchester, Essex. The fact that the backplate (not shown) of this clock is beautifully engraved, as many are, must surely indicate that it was *not* designed to stand on a bracket or mantle-piece with its back to the wall, when that engraving would be totally hidden, but rather to stand on a table, where the beauty of that costly back-plate could be seen through the glazed rear door.

It is a striking clock of 8-day duration with an optional strike-silent con-trol in the arch. The dial style is broadly similar to that of a longcase clock of the same period. A slot aperture below the XII allows a disc to be seen swinging with the beat of the pendulum. The case is of walnut. This clock is in the fine collection of Mr Bernard Mason, whose years of researches have discovered close on 400 examples of clocks made in Colchester. We have already discussed the scarcity of these costly spring-driven clocks, and this is emphasised by the fact that Mr Mason has traced only *five* examples of this type of clock made before 1750 in Colchester. It is not insignificant that Dammant's output was largely of the more costly type of clock, indicating that his customers were mostly in the higher income groups.

Dammant was born in 1683 and died in 1738. Dammant is one of those immigrant names to be found amongst members of the Dutch Church, in whose records the Fromanteels appear, though in fact Barnaby himself was not a Dutch Church member.

Hedge–Colchester (p 141)
Wall dial clock of about 1770 with 15in silvered brass dial. It is spring driven and of 8-day duration. The single winding hole indicates that it is a non-striker. The minute hand looks as if it may well be a replacement.

The Art of Makeing Clocks and Watches (p 150)
This print, here reduced from the 9in × 7in original, was made to illustrate an article on the trade in the *Universal Magazine* in 1748. Apart from the technicalities of clock layouts, hanging threateningly over our watchmaker's head, the print holds a degree of interest for the more general reader. On the wall by the doorway is a clock of the Act of Parliament type, made fifty years before the Act. Next to it is a rather grotesque longcase clock (marked *fig 6*). Apart from being stylistically a most unusual clock, this print betrays the unfamiliarity of the artist or engraver with clocks. The case has a most peculiar hood, the like of which I have never seen in reality. It has neither feet nor a plinth, but more serious is that it has no door and therefore no means of access.

This man, looking rather uncomfortable in his voluminous robe, frilly cuffs and wig on a somewhat bandy-legged chair, is apparently a watchmaker, as he seems to have no clock parts on his bench. Notice the glass bells to keep the dust out of his dismembered watches and notice too that he is surrounded by small tools, apparently mostly files. He seems to have no wheel-cutting engine and none of the heavier-duty clockmaking tackle. He is reminiscent of an eighteenth-century Robert Grinkin! Did watchmakers really wear this sort of dress for working, or has our artist put him in his Sunday best for the benefit of genteel readers?

BIBLIOGRAPHY

Baillie, G. H. *Watchmakers and Clockmakers of the World*, 1969
Beeson, C. F. C. *Clockmaking in Oxfordshire*, Ramsgate, 1967
Bellchambers, J. K. *Devonshire Clockmakers*, Torquay, 1962
——. *Somerset Clockmakers*, 1969
Bird, A. *English House Clocks*, Newton Abbot, 1973
Brown, H. Miles. *Cornish Clocks and Clockmakers,* Newton Abbot, 1970
Bruton, Eric. *The Longcase Clock*, 1970
Cescinsky, H., and Webster, M. R. *English Domestic Clocks*, 1913, repub 1969
Edwardes, E. L. *The Grandfather Clock*, Altrincham, 1971
——. *Weight-driven Chamber Clocks of the Middle Ages*, Altrincham, 1965
Lee, R. A. *The First Twelve Years of the English Pendulum Clock*, Byfleet, 1969
Loomes, Brian. *Lancashire Clocks and Clockmakers,* Newton Abbot, 1975
——. *The White Dial Clock*, Newton Abbot, 1974
——. *Westmorland Clocks and Clockmakers,* Newton Abbot, 1974
——. *Yorkshire Clockmakers*, Clapham, 1972
Mason, Bernard. *Clock and Watchmaking in Colchester*, 1969
Peate, Iorwerth C. *Clock and Watch Makers in Wales*, Cardiff, 1960
Symonds, R. W. *Thomas Tompion; His Life and Work*, 1951, repub 1969
Tait, Hugh. *Clocks in the British Museum*, 1968
Tyler, E. J. *European Clocks*, 1968
——. *The Craft of the Clockmaker*, 1973

ACKNOWLEDGEMENTS

Author and publishers wish to express their thanks for the cooperation and assistance of the following, without which this book might not have been possible: to the Worshipful Company of Clockmakers for access to and permission to quote from their archives, and especially to C R H Cooper, Keeper of Manuscripts at Guildhall Library and to Colonel H Quill, Honorary Surveyor of the Company, for their patience with my enquiries; to Mr L F Miller, co-author of *Suffolk Clocks and Clockmakers*; to my friends, Brian Morison and David Barker for their usual support; to my colleague, Peter Nutt, who again has persevered in helping to uncover new genealogical information; to R Sharpe France, Lancashire County Archivist, for permission to quote from documents in his care; to the Welsh Folk Museum, St Fagans, Cardiff, and to the National Library of Wales, Aberystwyth, for help with Sam Roberts's notebook and the photograph of his clock no 265; to Canon H Miles Brown, author of *Cornish Clocks and Clockmakers* and to J H Pethybridge for assistance with the notebooks of John Belling; to Mr E J Tyler, author of *European Clocks* and *The Craft of the Clockmaker*, for encouragement and assistance; to Mr E L Edwardes, author of the standard work, *The Grandfather Clock*, who has so patiently tolerated my many enquiries; to Dr John Penfold, author of *Cumberland Clockmakers*, for the same; to Bernard Mason, OBE, author of *Clock and Watchmaking in Colchester* for assistance and for kindly permitting me to use plates on p 122 and p 141 from his collection; to Dr R Plomp, the first man to publish accurate biographical information on the Fromanteels. Mr N Bestwick supplied the information on Wolley of Codnor; Mr Henry Ecroyd supplied the letter from his ancestor about a faulty watch.

In addition to the above thanks are due to the following for permission to use photographs of clocks in their possession: M P O'Connor, plate on p 20; the Knebworth collection, plate on p 33; Brighton Museum, plates on p 92 and p 93; Brian Morison, plate on p 171; David Barker, plates on p 127 and p 168; Fran Goodwin, plate on p 98; Alan Cheesebrough, plate on p 110; Keith Watson, plates on p 137 and p 175; Kenneth Rice, plates on p 134 and p 178; N Geary & Sons Ltd, Antique Dealers, Stanningley, Leeds, plate on p 129; Sidney Ireson for plate on p 94.

INDEX